BREAKING THE SILENCE

A Journey Deep Inside the Mind

DARA SANANDAJI

Dedicated to all those who suffer,
and to all those who hope

CONTENTS

BREAKING THE SILENCE

FOREWORD

There is no easy way to begin what I am about to say. But as is the case with most matters of the heart, beginnings are quite irrelevant.

It is a popular misconception that our journeys through personhood start at conception and that we individually carve our own paths throughout life to eventually hit a dead end with our last breath. The real truth is that our lives are simply a collection of inevitable reactions to varied external stimuli. What we have done in the past was already done for us before we did it, and what we will do in the future is what we would have done anyway.

But we still need not throw up our hands in defeatist frenzy. For, past and future are only illusory constructs. They are nothing but conceptualizations which help our brains make sense of the world we live in so that we can function within our environment. In fact, every moment in time is at a continuous crossroads of infinite states of being.

So in the end, we do have a choice. We have a choice as to how we think and act in the here and now. In essence, we are all choosing which one of our many lives we want to live at this very moment.

If by now you've come to the conclusion that this type of thinking is a step or two off the beaten path, well, you would be right. And I'll tell you why...

CHAPTER ONE

Duality Developed

MY CHILDHOOD WAS BOTH NORMAL and extraordinary. From what I remember as a young boy, I was cared for, nurtured, and given all the best stuff money can't buy. I wore footsy pajamas and carried my trusty, worn safety blanket. I sported homemade Halloween costumes and hunted for sweet prizes hidden within colorful eggs. I struggled with my R's and slurred my S's.

And I was taught. Boy, was I taught. I learned numbers, colors, shapes, and words—all kinds of words, including their prefixes and suffixes. I read *The Berenstain Bears* and Dr. Seuss. I learned Aesop's fables and played memory games. And this was all well before I even got to kindergarten.

As I began school, I was rather shy around the other kids at first. I have to admit, I wasn't sure what to do when the girl sitting next to me threw up all over my lap in first grade. But I soon began to make friends, and when we moved to another town after second grade, the summer days were sunnier and the winters were more crisp and refreshing. We played pinecone soccer before classes in the morning and tossed around the mini-football at recess. I was pulled from class often—not because of disobedience, but rather to attend the gifted programs at the school. I felt in control, ahead of the game, and part of a group. The academic success continued throughout junior high, along with a little extracurricular flare. I squeaked and honked on my older brother's saxophone in band and started a locker-organizing business and a lemonade stand with a friend. And I somehow snuck onto the basketball team, standing a towering 4'10" and a meaty 90 lbs.

But I certainly had the mischievous side as well. I became infatuated with the power of the curse word. When we moved to our new home, my mother had the good fortune of finding the bottom of our bunk bed tagged with every dirty word in the book, and then some. I rigged the phone so I could listen in on my brother's calls, and I learned how to pick the locks to all the doors in the house. And I prank called many, many people.

Then came the "cool" phase. It wasn't enough to be the smart kid in class. I had to know the right music, whip out the right sarcastic quips, and of course, I had to hang out with the coolest kids. Unfortunately, that meant neglecting some of the best friendships I've ever had.

And as I grew older, my desire to be in the "in-crowd" strengthened. I figured that this was not only a good way to be at the top of the social ladder, but that it was probably the best way to get girls to like me as well. Eventually, smoking and drinking took hold while I tried to climb my way to popularity.

Then, as high school progressed, I developed a sort of "duality," as one friend would later describe it. I maintained friendships with the kind and responsible kids during the Honors and AP classes in school, only to transform into party-boy mode on the weekends. They were two distinct attitudes, two personalities, two wholly separate perspectives.

Soon, though, the pecking order caught up with me. And when it did, it was not a pretty sight. Once the name-calling started, it was impossible to stop. At first, it would be just a casual dig here and there, but when the boys all got together with barrels of beer, one heckle turned into a few shouts. Then the shouts turned into chanting, and it was downhill from there.

No matter how angry I got, no matter how much I shouted back, the numbers were stacked against me. The name stuck. But I kept showing up at the parties, and I kept enduring the chants and the ridicule. I had too much damn pride to let it go. And I was too insecure to leave.

The hardest part was that many of the guys were friendly and nice most of the time. We would drink, laugh, play cards, drive around town, and shoot some hoops on the weekends, and I felt included for the most part. It was like a wicked pendulum, a Jekyll and Hyde world. But I endured and soon went off to college, hoping to move on to bigger and better things.

It was different out there. A new part of the country brought unfamiliar territory. The mentality wasn't the same. The world had expanded drastically. People were really smart—much smarter than I gave them credit for in many instances. But the tragedy of it all was that I dragged so much of the baggage I had had from high school with me to the college social scene. For some stupid reason, I thought that mimicking the part of the crazy high school cool guy would translate into being popular and meeting girls in college as well.

As I got drunker and stupider, I began to let one side of me wash away the other. My grades began to slip, and I didn't think much of it. It was hard to think at all sometimes with such a wicked hangover.

Unsurprisingly, the loud and obnoxious high school act soon wore thin with my good friends as well. I was so wrapped up in myself that I couldn't see that it was my self that I was really losing. Bitter and jaded, I became isolated. And what's worse, it took years after college to even begin to comprehend why people hesitated to gravitate toward such a rude, sarcastic, self-involved, and immature young man.

After I came home for the summer following my junior year, though, things began to look up a bit. A few friends from high school were still in town, and the name-calling had pretty much subsided by then. I played a lot of golf and looked forward to a new start and a last chance in my senior year.

Ready to head back to school, I packed up the car and rolled out of the driveway, not having any idea what lay ahead. In the middle of my solo road trip across the country, I stopped by a friend's university to spend a night or two before heading off to my own. Two nights turned into four, and I had to make it to the college the next day to enroll in classes. So I plopped down on my friend's couch, ready to dream of a glorious senior year. And then it hit.

CHAPTER TWO

Seeing Red

MY HEAD WAS STILL A BIT CLOUDY from the pot we had smoked earlier that afternoon, and I was having trouble sleeping. As the hours passed, a form of delirium began to set in. I stared at a hanging poster on the wall and fixated on the shadow cast by one of its curled corners.

"Did it move?" I thought to myself. "Not sure."

Then came the whispering. I could hear people talking, but I couldn't hear voices. It was as if I were reading aloud to myself in my head. But it wasn't me doing the reading.

"How is this happening?" I thought. "Well, if it isn't me, then it must be someone else. I'm in a room alone, but I'm between two other occupied rooms. Seriously? Can my friend and his roommates be communicating with me telepathically through the walls?"

And that's how it started. Intermittent conversation throughout the night kept me up. Because most of the thought communication involved telling others to shut up because people were trying to sleep, I didn't get up to wake anyone out of bed.

But eventually I had to try to clear my mind. I went out back a few times for a smoke, and the thoughts began to race around.

"How is this possible? Can other people out there communicate telepathically? How deep does this rabbit hole go?" I still couldn't sleep, so I went out again for another smoke. I accidentally closed the door behind me. I turned back and tried the handle: locked. Unfazed, I took a seat on one of the patio chairs on the porch and continued to think.

As dawn broke, novel concepts and innovative ideas began to pop into my head. And they were coming quickly. The nature of good and evil struck a particular chord. Then came the symbols. With nothing but a deck of playing cards in front of me, I began to reconstruct the world. Humanity began to flow through the cards.

"The dichotomous human experience is surely red and black in nature. Hearts are red for a reason. And black is the absence of light."

The concepts of love and hate had now become branded indelibly into my conscious thought.

"And let's not forget that most of the cards have numbers. Certainly they must mean something. I mean, what is that '8' if not just a 90-degree turn from the infinity symbol?"

So I had begun to figure it out. Each new discovery served to feed the presumption that I knew something others did not. And I liked that. The thoughts continued to circle more quickly, and I became more and more excited with each investigative success.

I paced around outside throughout the early morning hours in my socks, completely oblivious to my prior plans. What I was doing at the time was certainly more important. Then something else came to mind.

"What if others are listening? If there's a psychic battle between good and evil taking place, then I'm right in the middle of it. I'd better get into the house and reevaluate."

After pounding on the back door for a while and receiving no answer, I decided to head out on foot. The lines were drawn, and I needed to get to a safe zone—quickly.

Fearing the worst, the thought cycle turned sour.

"They're coming to get me, and I have nowhere to go."

Just then I remembered a house I had been to the night before. I had been hanging out there with a girl. But could I remember how to find it? The memory was hazy, but I didn't care. I just had to get there.

So I started running. How I found that house I'm still not sure. I could hear music playing inside. I knew the song well, and at that moment, I realized that it was definitely about me.

I knocked on the door, but no one answered. Shortly after, one of the girl's roommates came home. I pleaded for a place to sleep for a couple of minutes. I explained that I was locked out, hadn't slept all night, and couldn't find any of my friends. I'm pretty sure I was shaking. She let me in, gave me a blanket, and offered her couch.

As I walked into the common room, I saw something amazing. The whole wall was red.

"This is bigger than I thought."

I curled up on the couch and tried to sleep the frightening thoughts away. Nothing doing. After a while, I remembered my classes and figured that I had to make it out of there, one way or another. I popped up, bolted out of the house, and booked down the street. I got to my friend's house and knocked on the door. No one home.

As I turned around, I saw him coming up the street. He explained that he didn't know where I went and that he had left a note for me. Written on it were directions telling me how to find a key to the house on the back tire of his car.

Oblivious, I asked him if I could find a place to sleep for a while before I got back on the road. He also gave me a blanket and offered his room. After he headed back to class, I tried again, but couldn't sleep. The thoughts just kept racing.

When my friend came home after class, I asked him if I could take a quick shower because I had to be on the road soon. I heard the whispers again in the shower. "Now I've really got to go," I thought.

I slipped some hearts playing cards into their silverware drawer for their benefit, and to let them know that I knew. I grabbed my golf clubs, and as I was making my way out the door, I had one last word for my friend—"Reds." He would know what I meant.

As I headed down the street to my car, I passed by a pizza place. The doors were wide open. I could hear a woman talking from inside.

I heard her say faintly, "He's special."

I thought about it for a second.

"I must be projecting some kind of aura that I'm not aware of."

Then, as I turned the corner, I saw a military man in fatigues walking across the street.

"This is getting way too intense."

I chucked my bags in the car and sped off. Having no real sense of direction, I made a few wrong turns. The neighborhood I found myself in was pretty rundown, but I knew I'd make it out fine. As I turned off a rugged dirt road, I saw an arrow for an on-ramp to the highway. I immediately turned toward it, and when I saw a familiar sign, I knew I was on the right road.

Thoughts continued to pop.

"If military intelligence knows about the telepathy, then this is really big. What if aliens with the same—no, more advanced—powers are contacting us? I mean, bats have antennae and sonar capabilities. Bees and ants also have antennae. Plus, they have drone workers that communicate mysteriously with the queen. Is this the evolution of telepathy? Is there a sophisticated alien race, developed from similar-type animals, that is watching us from afar?"

Just then I hit some serious traffic. I had been slowed down. I wasn't supposed to be thinking about the aliens. As I looked down at the dashboard, I noticed that I was running low on gas. I pulled over next to a red car at the station.

I got out of my car, and the woman pumping gas into the red car looked at me and said aloud, "[This state] loves you!"

I was known all over, and I was doing something incredible. I was someone who could save the world. I got back in the car and kept driving. The music I was playing in the car made perfect sense. It was not only about me, but it was teaching me who I really was. Everything was in sync—the music, my actions, my surroundings, everything. This was real life.

I began to think about my dualities. I had to bring the two sides together into one coherent whole. I had to take the good in both sides and unite them. I thought about my family and how I had done wrong by them over the years. I sent out my apologies and my true feelings for them telepathically in the midst of a barrage of tears. I knew it would get to them. I kept driving. My red lighter would keep me safe from the evil I knew was coming.

As I stopped to stock up on some more bottles of red juice, I saw him. A portly young man with long hair and a baseball cap walked up to the entrance beside me. His evil was pure—he was an incarnation.

I looked at him with fear and condemnation, and he said aloud, "Dude, I'm just fat."

I walked past him quietly and looked suspiciously around the store. I hurriedly purchased several more bottles of red juice and tossed them into the passenger seat. At the next stop, I bought some cigarettes.

The clerk counted the change and said aloud, "Hey, 21!"

I took the two dimes and one penny he handed me and knew that luck was on my side.

Night fell, and I needed more cigarettes. As I looked over the opposite side of the highway, I noticed a red neon sign hidden by a few trees. The sign slowly became clearer, but I could still only make out the first two letters through the thick brush: "*HI*."

I had arrived and was welcome.

I made it to the front door of the restaurant, hoping to find a cigarette machine. Just as I opened the door, I saw a young boy fall to his knees. He collapsed as if in a moment of spiritual exasperation, almost overwhelmed by an answered prayer. I knew it had something to do with me. I slipped into the bathroom and waved my unlit red lighter back and forth to ward off the evil minion of a few flies.

Back on the highway, I knew morning would be coming soon, and I hadn't slept in I don't know how long. I had to get to a hotel. I looked to the right, and just then one popped out at me. I pulled in. After paying at the front desk, I made my way to the hotel room door. I looked down and noticed a newspaper on the ground in front of me. I picked it up and saw a picture of a large crowd on the front page. All of the people in the picture were reaching to the sky gloriously beneath the headline "*Let the Healing Begin!*"

"My sentiments exactly."

I jumped in bed and tried once again to sleep, but the thoughts were too fierce. I got up and looked in the closet to see what might be hidden there. A spectrum of light flashed by. Things were getting interesting. I turned on the television and flipped through the channels, landing on a late-night talk show. I couldn't believe what I was hearing. The monologue smacked of references to my situation.

"How does the host know what's happening to me? Are there cameras in the room? Can they see me through some medium unknown to most people, like light beams?"

I checked the bedside lamp.

Morning broke, and I was still conscious.

"Enrollment was yesterday, and classes start tomorrow. I really have to get back on the road."

When I jumped in the shower, I could hear the all-too-familiar debasement, loud and clear.

"PERVERT!"

This was no whisper. It was someone's voice.

"Where could this be coming from?" I wondered.

I looked down at the drain.

"This telepathy thing is clearly not limited to close proximity," I thought.

I had to continue to figure things out. So I packed up once again and headed out. But before I left, I slid a necktie and a shoehorn in between the doors to the adjoining room. My brother would need it, and he would know why.

Back on the road, I noticed a sign for a big metropolitan city. I needed to go there. I didn't know why, but I felt that there was something there for me. I made my way onto the exit ramp, followed it down, and pulled up to the stoplight next to an idling truck. A man inside rested his arm on the window. As he pulled his arm back into the car, I picked up a tracer that followed his motion.

"Whoa."

This guy's movements were so quick that I could only see a flash of color from his shirt.

"He must be one of the aliens."

Time to make a decision. I abruptly yanked the wheel to the left, parted ways with the alien man, turned the car around, and got back on the highway to school.

My stash of red juice was running low, but I knew I would be at school soon. The excitement grew. My aura was aligned perfectly with the beat and rhythm of the songs, and the words meant more. I could feel my heart beating out of my chest, my palms went cold, and my hands were light as a feather. I was in the zone and loving it.

I pulled into campus, windows down, music at 11. The sun was shining, people were smiling, and I waved to passersby who knew I had arrived. When I got to the fraternity parking lot, I jumped out of the car. And I danced. I just danced.

In the middle of my jam, I heard a voice calling out to me from up above on the second floor.

"Are you dancing?!" a friend of mine bellowed down from the window.

The music still blaring from the car, I began to toss the empty bottles of juice over my shoulder into the dumpster on the lot. The swarm of bees posed no problem to me, and even I was surprised by my incredible dexterity and coordination.

Soon after, a few of my good friends came out of the house and approached me. With a wide brimming grin, I asked one if he wanted to see how I could turn hate into love.

Taken aback, he said, "Sure, let's see it."

I looked around and found a car with a covering of dust on its trunk. As I began to write the word "*HATE*" with my finger, my other friends intervened. They asked what was going on and seemed surprised and concerned.

Just then I spotted a black pickup truck at the end of the lot with a decal on the back window. On it was a picture of a few cartoon characters and the phrase: "*South Mars*." I pointed at the truck, shouted, and moved toward it trying to show them what I knew.

A burly man immediately popped out of the truck and barked out at us menacingly. My friends assured him I wasn't trying to pick a fight and summarily diffused the situation. As my friends held me back, I shut down. My mind told my body to go limp, and I did. But I never hit the ground. They caught me and pulled me back up, and I went inside.

I bounded up the stairs to the second floor looking for the friend I had visited a few days before. I was sure he was there waiting to surprise me.

I could hear the voice aloud in my head again: "PERVERT! PERVERT!"

I checked the closet with the dog food. Then the second-floor balcony. Nope.

I ran downstairs to assess the situation. Soon after, campus Safety and Security showed up. As I spoke to some friends with a frenzied tongue, a crowd began to form. I noticed one of the female officers standing off to the side. Her eyes were aglow, and she shot me a knowing smile. I pointed to her eyes and tried to express that connection to the crowd.

I could hear murmurings when a uniformed police officer showed up at the front door. I confidently strode out to the porch to meet him, a half-bottle of red juice still in my hand. But before he could even begin an investigation into the commotion, I asked him if he wanted to see a trick. He humored me, and I flipped the open bottle in the air. I could see it falling in slow motion as it sailed past my open palm and landed splat all over the officer's immaculately shined shoes.

He grabbed me, spun me around, and with the assistance of another officer, slapped cuffs on my wrists behind my back. Many of my friends pleaded with the officers not to use force as they dragged me across the lawn to the squad car. I frantically tried to persuade them to enter the church next door, but they were strong and unwilling, and I was cuffed.

The officers asked me if I had been taking any drugs, and I thought to myself that this might actually be what an acid trip is like. I told them that it was possible that one of my friend's roommates could have slipped some acid into my drink at one of the parties.

We drove to the hospital, but certainly not in silence. I tried to make the officers aware of my incredible newfound knowledge by shouting out the colors and words on the street signs. They weren't getting it.

Out came the stretcher. The handcuffs turned into shackles, but again, I wasn't worried. I knew I could escape. Some attendants wheeled me into a small room on the ground floor of the hospital. I looked up and noticed a square light in the ceiling above. Family was watching me up there.

"Maybe I can transport into the light."

I tried, and in the midst of that effort, in came a man with a white coat and a pill. His motions were direct and decisive. He attempted to force the pill into my mouth, and I resisted. I could see the anger in his eyes. The forces of evil were at work again. I spit the pill out and tried to hiss the spirits away. He left the room.

I looked around and could see a dry-erase board through the doorway at the nurse's station. The words were written in red. I began to shout. I knew what was happening, and everyone could come out now. The jig was up.

A friend of mine from the fraternity walked in and asked me if I was alright. I told him not to worry, and that if he wanted to, he could kiss me. It would show him that I accepted him and that he didn't have to be afraid anymore. I had come to understand that nonsexual affection between men can be communicated, and that even homosexuality is not to be feared.

Surprised and perplexed, he laughed and also walked out of the room. I tried to Houdini my way out of the shackles, but the mad doctor interrupted me and was eventually able to stick me with a needle…

I awoke to heavy eyes. The bed was comfortable, and the room was warm.

"Am I on the moon?"

A young lady was sitting on a chair in the open doorway quietly reading. I rolled over to see where I was and noticed one green and one orange light on the hospital equipment. I asked her why the lights were those colors, and she asked me to try to rest. I kept asking questions.

"Where are we? What are you reading? Why are we here?"

The answers weren't coming. But what I did know was much more important than what I didn't.

Over the next few days, a team of doctors and interns would ask me long lists of questions. They seemed kind, but I knew that I had to hold most of my knowledge close to the vest, lest the evil come out of men.

My parents showed up the next day. They had been planning a thirty-year anniversary trip abroad around the same time, only to be blindsided by what was going on with me.

My mother would bring me crossword games and jigsaw puzzles to pass the time. Although I knew that the magazines in the hospital room were about me, I thought better about divulging that information to anyone.

I looked down at the bracelet on my wrist and saw a series of numbers. I snatched up a piece of scratch paper and scribbled them down. This code had to be cracked. Some simple math and branch diagrams later, the final answer jumped off the page at me. I had no doubt in my mind I had it right. The solution: an easy, straightforward, and glorious "1."

The doctors saw the etchings and were confused, so I downplayed the magnificent results. Then, when we had our next conversation about my thoughts and feelings, one of the doctors wrinkled his brow and asked me a very serious question: "What planet are we on?"

Without hesitation, I smiled and said, "*Third Rock from the Sun*."

It was then that I was introduced to the round pink pill. The doctors couldn't stress the importance of taking this medication enough. They would monitor the pill, its level in my blood, and my reaction to it, very closely from then on.

Throughout the next few days, the doctors and interns asked me the same question, listening intently with pens drawn and clipboards in place, awaiting my answer.

"How do you *feel*?"

The only word that would come to mind time and time again was, "Blah."

The pink pill, in concert with other pills and injections, had numbed my emotions. They pressed me for more explanation, but that's all I could think of at the time.

"Blah."

But the lack of feeling didn't curb my thoughts much at all. My world had changed forever, and my investigation had just begun.

After another day or two, I was transferred from the hospital to a friendly medical facility on campus reserved mostly for outpatient visits for students with common ailments. They gave me a spacious room with a television and access to a computer. I would be spending the next few nights there.

I turned on the television to see a familiar program. It was a quarter-century anniversary special for a long-running series. One of the comedians I knew best was performing in an old show that had been taped many, many years before. He had a still camera in hand and was aiming it at the video camera on set. As I paced around the room, his camera followed me and was snapping pictures of my movements.

"That's impossible—this show isn't even live!"

A whole new dimension had been added to the existing phenomenon.

I went over to the window and looked down at the parking lot. One of the doctors I had been seeing was searching around the lot. He came upon my car and peered in. Another person accompanied him, and together they glanced through every window. I was pretty sure they were on to something but still couldn't figure it out.

Later that day, I went outside to my car for a smoke, and my parents came out to meet me. Visibly shaken, my father asked what was going on. I pointed around the lot to all of the surrounding cars and asked them if they noticed anything in particular about them. They weren't getting it either.

Back inside, I wandered into the hall and noticed a large map of the country on the wall. Many colorful pushpins had been placed at various locations across the map. I found a red pin and confidently pegged my hometown. I would return later to see the red pin gone from my city.

"Cameras must be everywhere."

Later on, a friend came by with a video for us to watch in the common room. I didn't have much to say at the time. Things had gotten complicated. As we watched the movie in silence, the connections were zipping around. The movie's relation to my life had become too intense for me in that situation. I told her that I had better get some rest, so she left, and I returned to my room.

The next day, I worked on some breathing exercises with a gentle man in a cozy room.

"Visualize the breath entering the nose and filling the lungs," he said calmly. "Exhale fully and allow the breath to come back to the nose in a full cycle."

It seemed to make sense.

When I got back to the room, a pleasant woman in a colorful shirt appeared in the doorway. She sat down across from me and told me about her son. In a soft, comforting tone, she explained that he was about my age and that he played the guitar. It was clear. She was the reincarnation of a well-known folk musician who had died a few years before.

Then, in a more serious tone, she told me something that would return to me many, many years later.

"Stick around, you can help a lot of people."

The next day I was cleared to return to classes and began the process of selecting courses. I was able to move about a little bit more and tried to get settled in at the fraternity house. I asked a handy friend of mine to help me find a wooden board for the mattress in my room, and we went on a little road trip off campus to find one.

The music playing in the car once again matched up nicely with my thoughts. While driving, he mentioned to me that when he was with me, it seemed like he was in a movie. Things were becoming clearer every minute.

Back at the house, I was walking down the second-floor hall when I noticed something: the exit sign hanging from the ceiling was green and not the usual red. I mentioned the abnormality to my friend, and he shrugged.

I made my way into a friend's room where a group of guys were hanging out listening to music. I sat on the couch and explained to them that I was smoking the last cigarette I would ever smoke.

"Yeah, right" was the response.

I immediately jumped in again to explain, rather poorly and at a frenetic pace, potential synergies in aggregate human conduct. One of my friends, although clearly concerned, said that he kind of understood.

I then told them that I had found the best album ever recorded and asked them to play it. They weren't buying. What I failed to recognize was that my friends were calm, relaxed, and had chill music playing in the background for a reason.

I had to get back to the facility anyway, so I asked one of them if he could drive me over in my car, considering that the doctors had not cleared me to drive yet. Although a little uneasy not having driven much, he accepted graciously.

On my next trip back to the house, I walked the second floor again. I could hear shouting coming from the third-floor common room.

"It must be game day," I thought.

But this was no ordinary game. Every shout from above matched up with my thoughts and actions. They were communicating with me on a subtextual level. Many shouts of "N-o-o-o-o!" made me stop in my tracks and reconsider my thought process. A deep understanding of Earth's resources via alien involvement would have to wait, though. I had to get back to the facility again.

More thoughts poured in. The nature of man and woman flipped over into new discoveries in planetary motion. I had to show someone how this new scenario could play out.

With my mother and a doctor in the room, I decided to let them in on something that could change the history of our solar system. They listened intently as I took a handful of change out of my pocket. I began to place several coins of varying size in a straight line on the table.

I tried to demonstrate the potential for dual orbital paths for the first eight coins. As the *coup de grâs*, I explained that, under this scenario, the ninth coin becomes unnecessary. So I picked up the smallest and farthest coin and tossed it across the room.

“Hey, hey, hey! There’s no need to throw things around,” the doctor admonished me sternly.

He then ushered my mother out of the room, and in came a fresh cup of pills. By the time the wheelchair arrived, it was sorely needed. My head was an anvil, and my eyelids had magnetic energy. I resisted the forces valiantly, but in the end, gravity and magnetism won out. My head slumped down, and I was wheeled away. I would not be enrolling in classes that term after all.

CHAPTER THREE

Driving from Behind

MY FATHER AND I PACKED UP MY THINGS and got ready for the road trip back home. We couldn't fit everything in the car, so we decided that we would have to ship some of the items. We found our way to a local strip mall and parked in front of the shipping store.

Just as I was getting out of the car, an old beat-up sedan came roaring up beside us and skidded to a stop diagonally across two parking spots close by. A disheveled man popped out of the car and slammed the door behind him as he furiously hustled into another store. I could see that I was provoking powerful emotions in people.

I tried to calm my thoughts down as we entered the store. When everything had been rung up, the clerk chuckled lightheartedly. My father asked why, but I already knew. The clerk pointed to the register.

"$222.22!" he said smiling.

When we got back home, I was taken to a local hospital for evaluation. Shortly after I was admitted, a nurse approached me with a long, clear, rolled-up tube and a needle. She explained that they would have to put a dye in my blood so that a machine could pick up the activity in my brain. She needed my consent to proceed.

"Dye in my brain?!" I thought. "This might not be on the up and up."

I told her that I'd better wait to consult with my mother before we did anything like that. The nurse became frustrated and upset. She assured me that the procedure was routine and asked me several more times for my consent. I continued to decline, and she walked away in a huff.

"Not everyone is on my side," I figured. "I have to remember to be careful around here."

When my mother arrived, she confirmed that the procedure shouldn't be a problem. I told her about the nurse's attitude and likened her to a character in a well-known classic film. She got a kick out of that.

Soon after, some attendants lifted me onto a flat board in a room with a large picture window on one of the walls. As the machine rolled me headfirst into the tube, I could sense the doctors watching intently on the other side of the window. I heard a loud, piercing, buzzing noise and just tried to relax.

Images began to flash. Cartoon characters. But these were not the ordinary fuzzy visuals of amorphous dreams. They came to life in color, as if I were watching the television up close. Only I had my eyes closed.

Later on, when I sat down with the doctor, he asked me what I was thinking about when the machine was on.

I said calmly, "*Looney Tunes*."

The doctor let out a soft, kindly chuckle. But I wouldn't get this joke until the memory popped up years later.

I stayed on the same floor of that hospital for about a week. One of those days, an African American gentleman in a white coat sat me down to talk. He asked me about my thoughts. Just then a racist comment invaded my mind. I mentioned to him that I was having racist thoughts, but I made sure not to surrender my telepathic secrets. He shook his head in disgust and left the room.

Thankfully they had a smoking room on that floor—not just because I could get my fix, but also because I got to chat with some important people. One girl was an artist with an exotic name. In passing, I used a colloquial phrase about birds. She took issue with that, and I knew she was right.

"Animal life is indeed sacred," I thought.

And upon seeing her father, I immediately knew why she had objected—his beak rivaled the most statuesque of bald eagles'. That unsurprisingly triggered an internal dialogue about the evolutionary history of human beings.

Another man had been enduring severe shock therapy and was dazed most of the time. I felt for him because he seemed like a reasonable man. His likeness to my friend's father was unmistakable, and I knew that this encounter had to mean something. This hit home when I noticed his brand of cigarettes. I had never seen this type before. A large spade boldly graced the cover of the package. I was on the right track.

Outside the smoking room, an elderly African American lady sat down at the table next to me. She seemed aloof, but somehow lucid in a strange way. I knew she had been channeling some knowledge and was floating within those thoughts. When my brother visited me from work, I told him that I thought she was psychic.

He snapped his head back incredulously. "Psychic?!" he repeated.

I had faltered again, and I knew that I had to be much more careful with my knowledge from then on.

Later, I passed a tall, soft-spoken gentleman in the hall and struck up a conversation with him. As we walked into the common room together, he told me that he was part of a truck drivers' union. I remembered something. I ushered him over to the window and pointed down to the street. Across the highway was a sign on a building with some numbers and the word "*Local.*" I asked him if that was his union station. He seemed surprised but said that it certainly was. That came as no surprise to me.

I tried to pass the time by listening to my CD player, but the clock had slowed down considerably. I heard a loud humming noise coming from outside, so I went to the window. I could see a black helicopter setting down lightly next to the building. The government knew, and I knew that they knew.

My mother showed up toward the end of my stay, and by then I had been feeling cooped up and pretty stir crazy. The emotions intensified as I explained that I hadn't seen the sun in about a week. The tears began to flow.

My mother spoke to the staff, and they allowed me to take a supervised walk in the well-lit entrance hall downstairs at the hospital. The rays of light proved to be comforting and uplifting. I would be going home soon.

Back at my parents' house, I wasn't starved for distraction, to say the least. Music, television, writing, and deep thinking were some of my go-to activities. Mostly simultaneously.

And I began to paint. My parents bought me a large wooden easel, several kinds of brushes, large and small canvases, and, of course, a whole set of paints of all different colors. My creations were simple works of art, some may even say childish in nature. But they were meaningful, at least to me. And to my father.

He framed the two largest paintings, which were supposed to complement each other in symbolic relevance, and he proudly displayed them on a wall in the basement, along with a small representation of Earth's level system.

In another piece, I made the solar system more manageable for a viewing audience. I revisited my planetary alignment display, again with coins, but this time they were safely fixed in place with used chewing gum.

The weather was still amenable for golf, so I went out a few times toward the end of the season with my father. It was important to be outside. I sensed a newfound connection with environmental mythology and spirituality. Fire, water, earth, and wind—these were not just commonplace physical realities. We could utilize them, capture their energy, and learn the workings of the universe through them.

The wind picked up just as a player who was assigned to our group swung his club. The ball barely cleared the sand trap and landed softly on the green. I looked up at the puffy white images above as they slowly traversed across the pristine blue background.

"If I have these powers," I thought, "then there might be a few individuals or entities out there who can control the elements more than we know."

A friend of mine from high school joined me for another round of golf before the weather turned. Feeling an insatiable appetite for stimuli of any kind, I brought along my portable CD player and headphones. My father had purchased that CD player a little while before, and I certainly didn't fail to catch the likeness of a monkey carved within the lines on the front of the player.

"Yes, we undoubtedly have evolved much more than many people know," I thought to myself.

My friend seemed concerned at my insistence on hearing a few tunes in between strokes. I could tell he couldn't sense what I was sensing—all of this happening, all at the same time, all throughout the universe. It was too big to let go. Comfortable and normal daily interactions would have to take a back seat. At least for the time being.

A big New Year was coming up, and I knew something amazing would be happening. I called a friend who had been at the college for our first two years and tried to reconnect. I needed to go somewhere, and I only had a few options left.

Oblivious to customary social norms, I imposed on his plans with his friends from his hometown. I flew across the country and simply showed up at their hotel with no substantive planning. He had some idea I'd be there, but I hadn't really seen him much in the preceding few years. The awkwardness of flying solo and expecting a welcoming party was thick, but he played it down nicely.

We hung out to see some black shadowy figures rappel down a replica of a world-renowned tower right at the stroke of midnight. My bubble of expectation burst meaninglessly like the confetti poppers that littered the street. I headed back home shortly thereafter, still hanging on to a few remnants of anticipation for big things to come.

But after the holidays, it was time to go back to school. My room at the fraternity house had been vacant over the prior term, and you could tell. After I cleared all the cups, trays, and wrappers out of the room, a few friends helped me haul in a couch, a mattress, and a dresser. Our handyman friend also helped me install a wooden board to elevate the bed so I'd have more room. But this wasn't the raucous party I had been expecting the summer before by any stretch.

By then, the medication levels had stabilized, and its effects had taken hold. The "blah" emotional feeling I had described to the doctors had now spilled over into my cognitive thought process as well. I was static, baseline, zeroed out, almost robotic. To add to the mess, I knew that most of my friends had witnessed Act I. In fact, everyone on campus probably knew.

I lived just like I felt—a groggy morning, mundane class, lunch alone in my room, boring television, a semi-conscious nap on my couch, another monotonous class, more boring TV, an early night, and all over again. And it wasn't as if I couldn't hear the parties and the laughter bubbling up from the basement to the first floor below. This was an even harder pill to swallow than the round pink one.

I could sense that my friends were trying their best to be understanding, but I could also sense their desire to escape the contagion of awkwardness and negativity engulfing me. So I withdrew.

My investigative successes had turned out to be failings of the mind. I would helplessly look on as my lingering dream faded to black, and I would now have no choice but to accept my old sobering reality. But things would never be the same. The zest, spirit, and spice of life had been stripped from my consciousness. I had been emotionally lobotomized. The smell of the fresh-cut grass, which had always transported me back to the romantic daydreams of adolescence, had been completely neutralized. Walking into a familiar room with old friends had always lifted me into a zone of comfort, an understanding, a sense of who I was and where I was. Not anymore.

I blocked it out. If I didn't acknowledge it, it wasn't happening. I'd occasionally play some poker with a few of the guys, and going through the motions would have to suffice.

Over my next and last term at the college, I began to drink again now and then, attend some of the fraternity meetings, hang out with the guys, and try to recapture some of the old feelings. But forcing it was impossible. The glory days were gone for good.

Although I walked with my class on campus, I was still one credit short of my degree requirement. The empty tube I received from the gentleman on stage somehow seemed appropriate.

In fact, I almost missed even that. If a conscientious friend hadn't found me slumped in between my couch and coffee table the morning of graduation, it could have been a pretty bad scene. And it no doubt would have been a disservice to my family, who had traveled all the way out there to see me in the ceremony.

I returned home and took some classes at a local university over the summer to finally put a much-needed stamp on my college experience. The students in the classes were much younger than me, and the material was fairly basic. But I dug deep and dredged some energy out of the reserve tank that I could pour into my final attempt at academic redemption. I made my grades, although I knew very well that I hadn't exactly tackled quantum physics.

While at the university, I tried fleetingly to reconnect with a girl I had dated briefly the summer after high school. She worked there, and I figured that seeing her again might get me back on track a bit.

She was, as she always had been, incredibly kind and gracious, and she obliged to meet up. Selfishly, I couldn't even muster the graciousness of my own to give her the apology she rightly deserved. I had been nothing but rude and cold to her when I went off to school for freshman year several years before. I ignored her heartfelt emails and letters time and time again, and eventually, they just stopped coming. It was the worst in me, and I knew it.

But we still had lunch and went out a few times, and she mercifully didn't address my strange and awkward behavior. I don't know what I expected, but whatever it was, it wasn't going to work like that. We parted ways quietly, and I now had to face the cold reality of a difficult life that lay before me.

Many of my friends from high school had left town, and I didn't know many people from college who happened to be in the area either. Not to mention that I had managed to burn many of those bridges already, with either obnoxious or awkward behavior.

A couple of friends from high school were still around, though, and kindly looked past the weirdness to bring me along now and then to hang out in the city. When we went out, we would often go to the bars, and I began to drink excessively again. The liquid sledgehammer helped to numb the pain, and its inhibition-suppressing agent gave me carte blanche to be a little wild and crazy again.

But as I drank more and more, many of the old mental connections began to reappear. So pretty quickly, I began to realize that I wasn't completely off my rocker after all with my assessment of the red and black of the world.

As my friend and his other friends would mingle and talk to girls, I found myself doing laps around the bars, talking to bartenders, and taking careful note of my subtextual environment. Although I never relinquished my secrets, I still knew that I had the good in me and that it would inevitably prevail over the darkness.

So when I did have the chance to chat with random people here and there at the bars, the conversations didn't involve the typical flirtatious advances or common mating rituals. Instead, we talked about what really matters in life and how people are generally good at heart. We would chat about the nature of existence and the human condition. Although I was "35,000 feet in the air," as one friend would put it, albeit in a different context and many years later, I felt for the very first time that I could make honest and decent connections with other human beings in a substantive way.

But, as the liquor continued to flow, many other inhibitions began to wane as well. In particular, my libido, which had been starved for years, began to act up. Even though I was anything but suave with the ladies, and even though the nice guy never fared well at most of the bars we went to, I did have access to money.

One night I was at a fairly classy joint with a friend, and a woman discreetly waved us over to the table she was sitting at alone. We began to strike up a conversation. She seemed to be rather interested in me, especially when my friend left the table thoroughly unimpressed. It was one of the first times in my life that a woman had approached me openly and flirtatiously. Anywhere. After a few coy words, she asked me if I knew what she was.

I said, "Of course," not knowing what the hell she was talking about.

She asked if I wanted to leave the bar with her, and I gladly accepted the offer. We got in a cab, and not knowing where to go, I took her back to my friend's apartment in the city.

While in the cab, she was pretty forward to say the least, and I couldn't have been more thrilled. We went up to the balcony and tried the back door, but it was locked. Although she wanted badly to go inside, she acquiesced to hang out on the balcony.

When she asked for the money, I gave it to her without hesitation. The drink had done its job, and I had little fear or reservation. Right in the middle, though, we heard voices below in the parking lot. A few people were walking by, and without explanation, she jumped up and bolted down the stairs. She was gone, and my life would never be the same.

Although my friend almost always offered me a place to crash when we went out in the city, another inhibition would soon be overcome. I would often try to sleep, but the alcohol would keep me up. I would think about it for a second, but I'd inevitably make the split-second decision to jump in the car and drive all the way back to my parents' place in the suburbs. Speeding and music blaring, I would race down mostly empty highways during the wee hours of the morning. No awareness of circumstances. No thoughts of repercussions. No regard for safety. I was out of control.

Only looking back years later could I finally make sense of those dreams. Barreling down the highway in a swerving car, not able to see the bends in the road ahead. It was as if I were driving the car from far behind, almost like a video game. But the controller didn't work very well. And I knew the tragic end was coming soon. I would wake up before the climax and pass it off as just a stupid dream. But something would eventually click when they kept recurring mysteriously long after I stopped making the drives.

The next month, a few friends from high school were planning a trip to the city I had been to for the New Year's party the year before. Again, I managed to finagle my way into the plans, and we flew out together.

After some heavy partying, I got separated from the group. I sat down at a video poker machine and began to play. A young blonde lady sat in the seat next to me and asked me if I wanted her to suck my thumb. Again, unaware of what she was talking about, I just sat there while she took a twenty-dollar bill out of my hand and put it into the machine in front of her. Taken aback, embarrassed, and a little upset, I walked away and went back to the room.

But that got me to thinking. After most of the group came back and hit the sack, I stayed up and thought some more. I finally had some sense of what had transpired downstairs earlier that night. Then I came to a conclusion.

"I've already broken the seal, so why not?"

A little while later, two attractive young ladies came to the door of the hotel room, and I let them in. Again, right in the middle, one of my friends came in. I remember the embarrassment to this day, but strangely and sadly, that experience only served to foster and embolden my "why not" mentality.

Back home and seeking friendship, I tried to see if I could make any connections with people who were in town. I was able to reconnect with a cousin I had had some great times with as a young boy and who lived and worked in the city.

I had fond memories of summers playing tennis, interning together at my father's business, playing sports video games, and just being kids. But, although it was great to see him again, I'm pretty sure he realized right away that things were a little kooky.

One night after drinking heavily with other friends, I ended up outside the back door of a restaurant in the dark with another girl. Before I knew what was happening, my wallet and cell phone were gone, along with the girl, who had hopped in a cab down the street. I still had to find a way to pay the charge to the parking lot that was holding my car, but seeing as I was now broke, I had to make something happen.

I could think of only one place to go. Thankfully, my cousin answered the phone call from the front desk so early in the morning and sent a friend downstairs to lend me some money to get me out of the jam I had gotten myself into.

Later on, a friend from the old high school clique called me. He was looking for someone to hang out with, and it was another welcome opportunity for me to get out of the house. Because he had been bullied around by some of the same kids at school, we had something in common. Most of our other friends had found jobs and/or moved away. And especially when I had a falling out with the friend who used to host me in the city, I began to lean on this friend as a crutch for my only social option.

So we became drinking buddies. Being out all night and sleeping all day became the routine. But even though we would leave the house and drive to the bars together, we didn't have much to talk about when we went out. Most of what we had in common was that we had both chosen the same friends in high school. When we'd go out, I'd play the bar video games, we'd play some pool here and there, and we'd drink until late in the morning. I was living in a foggy daze, mentally and emotionally.

It had been almost a year since I walked with my class at graduation, and my parents began to press me about my work situation. I started to peruse the job market online, but I couldn't find anything I liked or that met my unreasonably high expectations.

I sent in to the college for a list of contacts from various industries, and I got back an extensive packet with names, phone numbers, and brief backgrounds. This service was no doubt a veritable gold mine, but I didn't even contact one reference. I was slipping into a comfort zone of dependence, and I couldn't see a good way out.

But just to go through the motions, I sent out several cover letters and resumés. As always, I knew how to go about the process better than anyone could ever teach me, so I would go it alone.

I got a few callbacks and gave some disastrous phone interviews, one in particular for a talent agency and one for a trading company. I didn't have any idea that the agency was one of the largest in the world, and my lack of knowledge about the organization came as a surprise to the interviewer as well. And I stumbled over a few mathematic riddles that seemed to crash and burn the trading interview as well. But one company did eventually invite me to come in for an in-person interview.

As I pulled off the highway and onto the site, I saw a huge factory-type building, but I couldn't see an address. I drove around back and found an entrance at the rear of the building. I walked through the door to find a dreary, dimly-lit office with some crammed cubicles and a greyish ambiance. Soon, a lady who worked there came by and brought me into a small room, where we chatted for a few minutes. She left the room for a while, and when she returned, all she said was that I was "overqualified" for the position. Disappointed, but also a little relieved, I made my way back home. More internet searching would have to do for the time being.

Meanwhile, I continued to go out with my drinking buddy. One specific night I will never forget. I had been downtown at a sporting event earlier that day with a friend I had known throughout school. She was a fun-loving girl, but nice and soft-spoken at the same time. We had been talking on the phone a bit, and I decided to ask her to the game. I wasn't sure if it would lead to anything, but I enjoyed her company and was always excited to see her.

I took her home after the game, and after I also went home, I got a call from my buddy. He asked me if I wanted to catch a big game on TV at a bar that night. I thought twice, but "why not" won out.

An early evening at the bar turned into a late night once again, and even then I wanted to continue the night. As I made a left turn onto a major road, my front left tire barely caught a rumble strip separating the two lanes of traffic. The tires squealed a bit as I made the turn. There wasn't enough air in them, and the angle was sharp.

Just then I saw the flashing lights in the rearview mirror. After much discussion and many tests, the officer shoved a breathalyzer in my face and demanded that I blow into it. I declined, and on came the cuffs.

License suspended and a hearing date set, my father picked me up and drove me home. I went through an exhausting trial process over the next few months, but after the judge watched the videotape of the roadside tests from the squad car that night, the verdict came in: "Not Guilty." Luckily, the records were expunged as well.

But I lost more than my license that night. When I told the girl I had gone to the game with about my predicament, she didn't have much of a response. I wouldn't see much of her after that.

I had to do something. I couldn't sit around all day just to wreck myself all night. Life was too short. So in a last ditch internet search, I found an application for an internship program in another major city. It looked somewhat interesting, so I gave it a shot and applied. It was time to start over again.

CHAPTER FOUR

Black, White…and Grey

I FLEW OUT THE NEXT MONTH and mentally noted the beginning of a new year and a fresh start. As I unpacked my things in a spacious fourth-floor apartment on a quiet tree-lined street, I marveled at the chance to finally live on my own. I would now be able to buy my own groceries, meet new and interesting people, be involved in a social scene, and begin an exciting career.

The director of the internship program had set me up with a position to assist a literary editor with research and fact-checking for a book. The author was an influential lobbyist who wrote extensively about pressing issues of particular public import. Although my tasks were mostly dedicated to researching global energy issues, my mind consistently wandered elsewhere.

The nation was just coming off the heels of an unprecedented and catastrophic historical event, and I was determined to get to the bottom of it. So, although I felt as if I completed most of my assigned tasks, I often used my time at the office to dig deep into the geopolitical history of a particularly heated conflict overseas.

One day I was printing some clandestine materials, and the editor happened to beat me to the printer. She snatched up my sheet, did a double take, shot a bewildered look in my direction, and replaced the paper on the printer. The awkwardness had followed me across the country once again.

The more my mind wandered, the more the thoughts began to race around. My importance to the structure and function of the world was being revealed to me again, albeit in a more refined fashion this time. Things had begun to pop out at me like before, but much more clearly and much more reasonably on this clip. I could begin to sense extraordinary significance in seemingly ordinary occurrences, and the snowball was already rolling down the hill.

Without a car, and having only the responsibility that comes with a part-time internship, I gripped the proverbial spigot of beer and yanked it to the left. I would mostly drink alone in the apartment, but when the liquid courage hit its threshold, I'd often venture out to the bar down the street.

I tried unsuccessfully to drag one of my good friends from college, who had transplanted to that city after school, along with me many times. But, unlike me, he had a serious job with plenty of accountability. And what's more, I could tell that he was, in any case, more than hesitant to partake in my quixotic escapades. Although we did take in a ball game and met up a few times, this would have to be by and large a solo mission.

One night I walked into the bar a few sheets in and stumbled upon a fascinating scene. The bar was packed, though I couldn't sense any of the bustling commotion, the boisterous laughter, or the shouting voices I was used to hearing there. I made my way to the back of the bar, where I would usually hack around on the pool table. I looked closely at the people around me. Gesticulations everywhere. It took me a while, but I finally got it.

I took a seat along the wall next to an attractive young Indian woman. I smiled at her and wrote my name invisibly with my index finger on the table between us. She smiled and did the same. I could see clearly now that not all communication requires the senses that most of us take for granted. But then again, I already knew that.

On another trip to the neighborhood bar, I puffed on a cigarette as I strolled confidently down the street. I soon crossed paths with a group of African American teenagers. I happily engaged them, and one of them asked me for a smoke. I popped open the lid to my pack and slid a cigarette out. Trying my best to play it cool, I flipped the smoke to her in the air. It bounced off her outstretched palm and fell helplessly to the wet ground below. I apologized and began to slide another cigarette out of the pack. Too late.

The shouting had already started. One thing led to another. A push, a shove, and then a sharp blow to the back of the head. I wheeled around and booked down the street as fast as my short legs could take me. Heart pounding and arms flailing, I shouted repeatedly for help at the top of my lungs. No one responded. The tree-lined street was as quiet as ever. Then I saw an elderly couple at the end of the next block. They seemed unfazed, so I stopped in my tracks. I turned around. The kids were gone.

At the end of the next block, I came upon a police cruiser and flagged it down. I recounted my story to the officers, and they radioed it in. One of the officers drove me around for a while to look for the group of kids when he got a call over the radio. We pulled up to the intersection where he had initially picked me up. Another squad car beamed its spotlight across to the other corner of the street. I could see all five kids lined up on the corner shading their eyes from the glare. The officer asked me if I could identify them and if I wanted to file a complaint. Although I knew it was the same group, I refused. Just getting home would be more than good enough.

The next few weeks seemed humdrum, at least on paper. Ordinary trips to the grocery store, the video store, and the dry-cleaner's were highlight activities. But as the weeks drew on, each event became more significant.

One day after I picked up a few things from the store, I passed alongside an African American gentleman on the sidewalk.

"That's funny," I thought to myself.

He was wearing the same maroon polo shirt tucked into the same color blue jeans as I was. I was just like this man, and I was only beginning to figure that out.

The next day I stood on my balcony pondering while looking out onto the street below. A lady was walking with several young children and teaching them about the flowers, the grass, the trees, and the sky. She raised her hands at the wonder that surrounded them.

A familiar thought popped into my head. This had something to do with me. But just then, the feeling turned sour. It was as if I were being spoken to in a soft, condescending tone, as if I were a child who didn't know which way was up. I thought about the man I had passed by earlier on the street, and it felt like a remedial lesson for something I already knew.

These countervailing forces battled one another fiercely throughout the next week. I was once again in the midst of an epic struggle, and I knew too much. I expended enormous energy trying to ward off unwelcome thoughts while attempting to referee others. The little work I was doing was suffering, and when I entered the office one day, a room humming with conversation suddenly fell silent. The pressure was building, and I had to get away.

I called my mother and told her that I wasn't feeling well. She suggested that I fly home and see the doctor who had been monitoring my medication. At the airport, I had to don my headphones to drown out all the chatter thrust in my direction. But it wasn't that easy. I saw some men looking toward me and could still hear them speaking in sync with my music, both in topic and time. This was all way too intense.

By the time my mother drove me to the hospital to see the doctor, the whispering had returned in full force. The people around me were communicating with me telepathically again. Most of the transmissions had negative overtones—I was being reprimanded most of the time.

And the whispering would match up perfectly with some activity that was going on around me, some thought I was having at that moment, or both. The frustration with the lack of control and the negativity was almost eclipsed by the specter of not knowing how it was happening.

While in the car, I let my head sink to my shoulders. Then I heard something. Loud and clear. A telephone was ringing. I could tell by the ring that it was a landline.

I heard my doctor answer crisply in my head,

"This is Dr.—."

Then the voice went silent.

When I finally got to see the doctor, I kept the discussion to my racing thoughts and nothing else. I knew what full disclosure would lead to, and I couldn't afford that again. He then introduced me to a large, round white pill.

I tried to get some rest over the next week, but the thoughts kept charging. My mother would bring me comfort food, but even that couldn't slow things down. She had to call the doctor again. He prescribed a much larger dose of the white pill, but it didn't knock me out right away. I stayed up most of the night unable to stop my legs from twitching and kicking. Finally the convulsing subsided, and I fell asleep. Over the next few weeks, the large doses of the white pill began to numb my thoughts.

And although I was finally cleared to head back to the internship, the editor had already written it off. I hadn't told them much about where I was or what I was doing and hadn't emailed with her in about a week. I was told that it would be better if I didn't return. Fortunately, the director of the internship program had another position available, and I flew back to the city to start over again.

I was in limbo. The white pill had begun to counteract my racing thought communication, but the collateral damage was my intellectual thought. I worked at a trade office that last month of the internship program doing mostly busy work for the institution. The lady who had basically created the position for me was friendly and amenable, and she welcomed me warmly into the office. My work there would end blandly and without incident.

As I was getting ready to head back home, I called my friend from college to chat before I left. We stood out on the balcony, and he asked me about my next steps in life. By that time, I was in a funk, and I'm pretty sure my cloudy haze was palpable. He asked if I had ever considered going back to school, in particular to law school. He mentioned that a degree like that could open a lot of doors for me. I respected his opinion, and I would think about that a lot over the next month or so.

Back home, I refined my job search and things became a bit more serious. I listed all the major law firms in the city, ranked them, and began to contact them one by one. Although I received no response from most of them, two of the largest and highest on my list did bring me in for interviews for entry-level, clerical-type positions.

"I might actually have something here," I thought.

I made my way downtown during the day in awe at the crowd of people hustling through the streets. The decisiveness and purpose with which the power suits strode in and out of the buildings began to inspire me. I found my way up the elevator onto a floor of pure busyness and sat down with a woman for a brief chat before she guided me into an office for a few tests. I whipped through the math test looking for my next conquest.

When she came back in, she handed me a sheet and asked me to type the words from the page onto the computer as fast as I could with as few mistakes as possible. I was no typist to say the least, but I tried.

"Time's up."

I had finished only about a quarter of the sheet, and it was pocked all over with typos and misspellings. Next interview.

As I found my way downtown the next time, I still didn't understand the job description for the position. I didn't even know what the title meant. But I summarily dispensed with the math test once again.

The next test, just like the previous interview, involved a sheet of paper with some writing. But this time I was to proofread the text and correct the errors with "common shorthand."

"What the hell is 'common shorthand'?!" I asked myself.

I corrected some of the misspellings and incorrect grammar by crossing out the words and rewriting the text in the margins. The lady came back, took the document from me, and left the room for a while. She returned a few minutes later quite perplexed.

"How do I apply to law school again?"

I purchased as many crash-course books and practice tests as I could find at the bookstore. I needed to ace the qualification exam, and I would put everything I had into it. Although time was an issue, I was testing quite high in practice. I was finally ready.

As I walked into the silent classroom, the butterflies began to flap their wings uncontrollably. But I knew I could do this. Three-quarters through the test, I felt pretty solid. I had answered most of the questions confidently and was on a decent roll. Then came the logic games. Moment of truth.

"A red car parks in spot 1 Mondays, Wednesdays, and Fridays. Car 3 parks in spot 4 on Tuesdays and Wednesdays."

And so on, and so on.

"What color is car 2 on Thursday, and what spot does the blue car park in on Friday?"

I had seen a setup like this before in the practice exams, and I knew I could solve every one of these. But would I have enough *time*? It was always about the time.

Looking back, I think the clock was kinder to me in practice. And the butterflies weren't flapping at home either. In any case, I was able to complete all the answers to only two of the four logic games.

"C, C, C, C..."

Unsurprisingly, my ego was black and blue after I saw the results on paper. And as always, I couldn't settle. The donkey in me had too much kick. I would sign up to retake the exam and prove my competence.

I had a few more months to grind again, so I would take dozens more practice tests to get the timing perfect. One day in the middle of practice, I got a call from an old friend I had known ever since we moved to my hometown.

We had been very close as kids, all the way up to my "cool" phase. But, just like some of my other tight friends from grade school and junior high, and just like the girl I had dated the summer after high school, I decided one day way back when that I couldn't know him anymore. "Unfair" is not strong enough of a word sometimes.

Even so, I'm sure he knew that I was down and out, and when he came back into town, he unflinchingly outstretched his hand. We searched around for a bit and eventually found a popular spot in the city where we could room together.

Only a few problems, though. A plethora of neighborhood dive bars lined the adjacent street, a delectable pizza joint graced a nearby intersection, and a "big-as-your-head" late-night burrito joint was only steps away. I hammered away at practice tests during the day, got hammered at the bars at night, and stuffed my belly into the early morn.

I could tell that my friend was becoming saturated with the noise at all hours of the night. It couldn't have been fun to constantly wake up early in the morning to witness a stumbling roommate, shirt completely soiled with dripping taco sauce.

At first, we would head out to the bars together, but even that stopped after a while. Pretty soon he would find work in another city, and my four-month jaunt downtown would come to an end abruptly.

But before we would move out, I would continue to focus on that exam. I even took the train downtown regularly to attend exam workshop classes, although they were basic in nature and didn't do much for me. It was still all about the time.

The second test was much better than the first, but I still couldn't finish that last dang logic game. So the day after the test, I called up and canceled the score reporting on the spot. Again, this would not do.

I felt that my performance on a third and final exam would eclipse both the first and the second, so I crossed my fingers and hoped for the best. The results came back: middle of the road.

"Maybe the admissions committees will just overlook the poor score and see that I have potential."

But even I knew that that was wishful thinking.

Recommendations in and essays completed, thirteen applications had been submitted. I obsessed about the three levels of rankings that I had categorized all the schools into. Probabilities of acceptance whipped around in my head.

Then I got something in the mail. I hadn't been expecting the application, but it was short and sweet, and it was a local school. It was ranked by the well-known publications lower than every one of the other schools on my list, but, "why not?" The school was in the city, it was a sure thing backup, and it was a quick application. So I filed it.

The rejection letters came in early and often. After all that, only two waitlists—one from a middle tier and one from the lowest. Then my backup's letter arrived. I was in. Waitlists expired, I enrolled for the fall, looking to ace the first semester and immediately transfer out. It was a foregone conclusion.

It was springtime, and I would still be idle until the fall. My parents didn't like the sound of that, so my father brought me into his office, and I reluctantly delved into some busywork. Uninterested and unmotivated, my full days began to get shorter and shorter, and the lunches down the street at the house got longer and longer. Eventually I just stopped going. I would be on my way back to the city again soon anyway.

By the time I enrolled in classes, the large, white round pill had taken hold in concert with the round pink pill. I was still quite numbed emotionally, and somewhat intellectually, although not as much as before. Over the preceding year and a half, most of the whispering and cosmic thoughts had subsided, and a sense of muted normalcy had settled in.

I walked into the first class with my nose in the air and left feeling confirmed. The students had been asked to introduce themselves and provide a little background about their lives. I was thoroughly unimpressed with the caliber of the undergraduate schools that my classmates had attended. I would just put up with the first semester, and then I'd be able find a more suitable place to study.

But as classes started, something shocking began to happen. The professors would ask questions of the class based on the voluminous reading material and the lecture topics. I was sure that I knew almost all the right answers, probably unlike many of my classmates. And when I heard the other students' comments, I once again felt confirmed. For the most part, I was confident that what they were saying was completely off base and made no sense whatsoever. They clearly had the wrong answers. Incomprehensibly to me, though, this was not how any of the professors were responding. Most of the time the professors would nod, commend them for a good argument, and proceed with the lecture, often utilizing the students' input in constructing further arguments.

"What the heck is going on here?" I wondered. "I must be in the damn *Twilight Zone*. I mean, these are questions, and they have answers. You analyze the problem, and you come up with the solution. How hard can it really be?"

To my surprise, my simplistic dichotomous world would soon be shattered. I quickly became engulfed in a universe full of blurry grey lines and amorphous shadows. Many of the lectures touched only briefly on the pure text of the readings. The tangents were deep and the hypotheticals plentiful.

As I had almost always done at every level of school, I took copious notes of everything the professors said. I scribbled furiously, but I was never able to keep up with the pace. I'd often lose place and not have any idea what I had just written nor have caught the pivot into the new discussion. I decided that I'd better stay quiet so as not to ask any stupid questions.

I would go home after classes exhausted but feeling that I could still handle the material. When I would read at home, I'd get it. I felt that I could understand all of the intricacies and nuances of the cases, and I'd follow the reasoning of the court's decisions to a "T."

But kryptonite would inevitably find its way into all my classes. I thought that if I studied alone and grinded through the case law, I'd still be able to ace the exams, given my perception of the relative talent level of the other students.

The writing class provided some promise as well. I had the luxury of going home and pulling all-nighters, poring over the cases, outlining arguments, and refining my text. I was confident writing, and I could follow directions. The formula for legal writing was organized and made sense. It was meticulous work, and I liked that. Certainly, my work would have to be the best in my class. Well, not quite. I did pretty well, but my argumentation skills were still lacking. I struggled with depth versus breadth issues and counterarguments. So no problem—I'd just have to ace all my core course exams then.

Thankfully, because the whispering had died down, I could focus most of my thoughts. I was basically on autopilot and had no time or energy to even consider the debacle of the previous four years since my episode in college. Because of that, I was able to make some good friends with some fellow smokers who would congregate in front of the building before and after class.

We would go out now and then, mostly on the weekends, but I think party-boy mode was a little much for some of them. It wasn't necessarily the excessive drinking in itself. I think it had much more to do with many of the unresolved psychological issues I had chosen not to deal with. Myriad insecurities and some particularly acute autonomy problems would simmer within my unconscious thought and would inevitably bubble to the surface every time we went out late. Although a few regrettable nights put a damper on some of my friendships, the kicker was still to come.

CHAPTER FIVE

Finding Meaning

EXAMS WERE NEARING, and the nights became longer and more grueling. My sleep schedule suffered. I endured a few all-nighters for my final legal writing memo and almost a full all-nighter for my first exam. It was not my best effort, but I thought I could still come out strong with the numbers.

Next exam. I was two more all-nighters in, it was past midnight, and the exam was the next morning. And I had only gotten through half the material. Not to mention that I hadn't even gotten a chance to look at any of the example exams which the professor had so highly recommended as the most useful study tools at our disposal. I wouldn't need them anyway. As long as I could memorize the law, I'd be fine.

Just then I felt it. Dizziness set in. I tried to fight through it. I read my outline out loud and tried to etch the text into my brain.

"What was that last line again?"

I had completely lost it. I read it three more times and put the paper down. No idea what I just read. It went on like that for about an hour or two. Utterly defeated, I slumped down on the futon and faded away.

I awoke a few hours later in a panic.

"I'll just have to push through this one and make it happen," I told myself.

I had never had this feeling before going into an exam. I was unprepared for many exams in college, but it was never this bad.

Books closed, the proctor passed out the fact sheets. I couldn't even grasp the concept of the exam.

"What are we supposed to write? I've never heard of any of these types of activities in the facts. How does any of this relate to anything I studied all semester? Where are the questions about the law?"

I just stared at the sheet in front of me. I read it again. Usually at this point, my adrenaline would kick in, and I would think of something. This time I was blank.

About an hour or so through the four-hour exam, I began to scribble some nonsense into the small blue book on my desk. I used some of my legal writing technique and discussed some peripheral issues that I forced into the discussion. Many of the facts went unaddressed, and I knew that that was a bad sign. As I had heard from someone earlier that semester, "Everything means something. It's all there for a reason."

I had a few more days to study for my last exam, and I knew I had to make this one count. I got a decent outline together after the first day or two, and I felt somewhat ready.

But what I didn't account for was the return of the whispering. And when it struck, it came charging in. Demeaning and baseless comments invaded my brain like a vicious virus. I fought them off with everything I had, but it was a losing battle from the start. Winning a fight is impossible if you don't know whom you're fighting, how, or why.

Somehow, I dragged myself into the classroom for the exam. I walked in to a steady buzz. Frantic students were nervously murmuring, shuffling papers, and excitedly debating last-minute issues. Then it came, not as a voice, but as loud as a thought can be.

"GAY! GAY! GAY!"

I wheeled around and calmly walked back through the doorway and out of the room. I would not be taking the exam that day.

I called my mother and got in touch with my doctor. As per his recommendation, I went into the dean's office to explain that I had a medical reason for not taking the exam earlier that day. He would need a doctor's note, and I would provide one for him. The dean was kind and understanding, and he and the professor both allowed me to take the exam a few days later. But by then my condition had worsened.

When I went in to see the doctor, he gave me a small white pill, which I would later refer to as "candy." I'm not sure why I called it that, but it went down easy nevertheless. He also upped the dosage of the large white pill and gave me a light pink pill for my nerves.

Heavily medicated, I walked in to the retake the exam. As I sat down at the desk, I felt strangely confident. But this wasn't the typical swagger I had brought to high school tests. It was more of an up–in-the-clouds kind of contentment with my abilities. The questions seemed straightforward, and my answers were brief and to the point.

"This law school thing might work out after all," I thought.

After exams, I was supposed to head out to an island vacation with my parents for a few weeks over break. Not only was I totally spent, but some of the thoughts from years past had started to creep in again as well.

There was a major conspiracy afoot. I would sense it in my dreams at night and try to piece it together during the day. The fate of the world was being decided. There was no way I could make this trip. My parents were understanding as usual and encouraged me to rest over break.

As the higher doses set in, I vowed to realize my full intellectual potential in the spring semester. I hoped that I could keep the invading thoughts at bay, at least until after final exams.

I settled in with my classes and did my best to read every case assigned. I would hold back as much as possible on the partying, at least for the time being, to focus on academic redemption.

But when grades from the previous semester were released, I had to take a moment to collect myself. I was close to the very bottom of my class, teetering on the precipice of academic probation. Although transferring was pretty much out of the question at that point, I knew that I had to make things right and get back on track.

So I studied. I began to learn how to think again, just not the way in which I was used to thinking. I found myself knee-deep in analogy, linguistic connections, new jargon, and perspective. Long gone was the mechanical mathematical model of thought. More importantly, though, long gone was any semblance of right and wrong answers. It was no longer about *what* your conclusions were. It was about *how* you reached them.

Although I had first conceptualized it as such, the law was not self-explanatory, rigid, or straightforward by any stretch of the imagination. It had now become amorphous and flexible, and most importantly, always open to different interpretations.

I also learned that brief and to the point was never a stellar way to tackle an exam. It was about issue spotting—a sort of *Where's Waldo* approach. And oh yes, everything did mean something.

It was typically a "kitchen-sink" mentality. It was a race to see how many legal issues you could effectively extract from the fact pattern. But of course, issue spotting was just the beginning. What would end up separating a good exam from a top-notch one would be the depth and quality of the arguments for each particular issue.

So I had learned the hard way that memorizing the law was not only futile, but that it was largely unproductive as well. What mattered most was not what you knew, but rather how you *thought.*

For the first time in my life, I had actually begun to use my brain. Throughout previous schooling, I had mastered the academic tricks of the trade via rote memory and regurgitation of factual information. I followed directions meticulously, and I always knew exactly what the teacher was looking for. And my timing was excellent. I knew how fast I had to solve problems, and my internal clock was hooked up directly to GMT. That did me just fine for most of my life.

But now I was forced to come out of that cozy shell and begin to truly and honestly think for myself. I wasn't being told what to do and how to do it anymore. No more neatly wrapped packages of compartmentalization, no more trusty stick-on labels, and no more hard-and-fast numbers. The world had expanded, the possibilities were limitless, and the universe was infinite.

The winds of change had swung open the doors to theory, philosophy, and notions of justice and principle. Rights required responsibility, and law was inextricably linked to morality. But I was finding much more than increased intellectual capacity here. I started to see nuance and subtlety all around me. And it wasn't just all around me—it was *in* me. I jumped in headfirst.

I studied more and drank less. Although this strategy seemed to be working for me academically, it also came with a downside. I began to lose touch with many of my smoking buddies. I withdrew in large part, and social discomfort set in.

The large white pill had also created a monster out of my appetite, and I had become literally too big for my britches. Many trips to all kinds of fast food joints helped to round out my puffy face and bloated gut. And unsurprisingly, my insatiable hunger for food mirrored the plight of my still-starving libido as well.

I opened the phone book a few times and made some calls. The ladies would come and go, but I was inevitably left alone and even less satisfied—mostly with myself. A few girls at the school did express some interest in me during my first semester, and some of that even lingered over to the second one. An awkward night with a pleasant girl in our circle of friends only served to muddle things even more. Enveloped in my own issues, I wouldn't see much of her after that.

One of the few nights that semester when I did go out with some of the guys, we ended up outside a nightclub and were approached by a few scantily clad women. I jumped at the chance to offer one of them a ride in our cab. The ride with the woman and my friend was largely silent. After we arrived at our building, we parted ways with my friend, but we all knew what the deal was. And now so did many of my classmates.

But I plugged onward, blocked out the mess, and tried to focus on the job at hand. I still enjoyed the legal writing, and after an exhausting appellate brief, I finally felt that I was actually somewhat present on my law school journey.

Then came oral arguments. Diligent preparation and some of the old butterflies—the friendly kind this time—would give me a little shot in the arm. I embraced the untapped reservoir of public speaking like never before. The bar was high, but I knew that I had enough spring to clear that hurdle.

So I continued to prepare. I would be arguing in front of a panel of three anonymous judges. The pool consisted of professors briefed on the case and some successful former students familiar with the arguments.

I knew that going up against talented classmates, many of whom already knew how to think, and many with deserved confidence and swagger, would be a tough battle. But I planned carefully, and our professor gave us plenty of opportunity to do some dry runs before the graded moment of truth.

Somewhat to my surprise, words actually began to come out of my mouth. And sometimes they even made sense. I would often be able to pick up a dipping curveball, give it a confident whack, pivot, and expound on my previous argument. I juked and jived through a pretty solid practice run.

It was amazing to me. I was still at the helm and hadn't completely wrecked the ship just yet. But although I could pick up a decent breaking ball in practice, I flew a little too close to the sun.

During the graded debate, I dug a nice deep hole for my adversary and deviously covered it with a makeshift patch of hay, hoping he would walk right into it. But he gingerly sidestepped the trap, and after an on-her-toes judge tossed me a wicked slider, I came up fanning air. I stumbled across the finish line, a little embarrassed and disappointed that I let one get away. But the grade was generous, and most importantly, I was making some solid progress.

When exams rolled around, I trekked through the sludge of a couple of core course exams. As always, the clock was a persistent and valiant foe. But I finally had some sense of how to write an exam, and I ended up well above mediocrity in the point department.

The last exam would be mostly theory and twenty-four-hour take-home. I hustled back to my studio apartment a few blocks away from school, already scanning the fact pattern while I made my way down the sidewalk. Twenty-three hours and fifty-eight minutes later, I slid my polished best effort under the professor's door.

This one was different. I had time. I could outline, erase, cross out, and draw lines, circles, and diagrams. I could manage the clock on my wall effectively. It was how things should be. It was right, and I was satisfied.

The professor docked me just two points, and I was only one point short of the coveted highest-grade honors, in one of the largest class sections we had first year. I couldn't see why I lost those points, but it would have to do. My comeback plan had been successful.

Pretty much the day I handed in that last exam, I began to feel a little strange again. I quickly began to slip down that cosmic rabbit hole I knew so well. Once more, hyperawareness of my external environment began to dominate my conscious thought. Colors were jumping out at me, and forces I couldn't see or hear were at work again. I didn't know how or why, but I just knew that something important below the surface was going on around me.

My promise to fight off the infectious virus that semester had been fulfilled, but my time was up. The whispering had returned for another heavyweight bout. But this time it wouldn't be just whispering I would have to deal with.

After exams, I decided to go out and have a few beers to unwind. I hadn't been drinking in a while, and as the semester had been a particularly long and grueling one, I needed a release.

About four beers in, I decided that it would be a good idea to roll around the club areas solo in a cab, looking for anything and anyone. I asked the cabbie to stop along a sidewalk.

As I got out of the car, I came across a pretty young woman walking by herself. I asked her unabashedly if she wanted to "hang out." Having the subtextual knowledge that I was being followed, I knew I had to make it quick. My suspicions were confirmed when a nicely dressed gentleman walked by us on the street and curled his lips into a knowing grin. The woman then asked me if I had any money on me, and I quickly produced the stash I had retrieved from the ATM moments earlier. We hopped back in the cab en route to my apartment.

She was a kind person, and afterwards we chatted briefly. She gave me her phone number and a warm embrace. The hug surprised me. In fact, this hug would affect me more than I could have ever imagined at the time. Over the next few days, my mind would race with possibilities. All negative. Guilt had arrived in spades.

“What the hell am I doing with these women? What if I catch something? What are the odds of that? What if they lie about what we did and try to sue me or something? What if their families find out and try to get retribution on me? How can I explain this if I ever have the fortune of meeting a ‘nice’ girl? What about the money? What if everyone finds out? What if my family finds out? A few people already know, and if more catch wind, I will be disgraced, humiliated, and shunned. What if the cops find out? Could I be arrested for this? What did we really say and do? What was the evidence? Even if I can’t be convicted, arrest would be damaging enough. What a total mess. I think I need to stop drinking completely and lock myself down for seven to ten years.”

Soon everything I had ever regretted or been ashamed of in my entire life began to flash into my mind. First, the close friend from grade school and junior high I had left in the dust all those years ago. We had done everything together. We constructed snow forts with cup holders. We designed, built, and painted a wooden chair in the garage. We played basketball and football. We skateboarded. And we made up and sang silly songs. We started to talk about girls, watched sophomoric television programs, and ate puffy cheese doodles with chopsticks. We were a team. But I just had to get on to more popular things, so one day I just stopped talking to him altogether. No reason, no explanation, just an icy shoulder.

Another close childhood friend—same thing. We had hung out together a little while longer than some of my other old friends, even a little in high school. We burned parchment to create an authentic school project, and we chatted with the teachers in junior high after school almost daily. One teacher even dubbed us “Frick and Frack,” “Peat and Re-Peat.” But high school would have to be every man for himself, a free-for-all of finding the coolest friends. We still hung out a little within the same circles at first, but things were never really the same.

I remembered one night when we were still young. We went out to a concert in the city. We had been drinking, and neither of us knew the city very well at that point. We were following some older kids on the train to the concert. There was some indecisiveness as to whether the next stop was the right one. The guys in front of us got off pretty much in the nick of time.

I just stood there as the doors began to close in slow motion. I could get through, but there was no way my buddy could make it. As the doors slowly slid shut, I had to make a snap decision. I jumped out. One of my closest confidantes, backers, and champions, through thick and thin, had been left behind alone on a train bound for nowhere.

Next one. After I shunned the girl I dated in high school, I immediately became interested in a girl at college. She was different, unique, and had a certain individual flare. I liked that. She could also keep up with the guys, and I respected that too.

I tried hopelessly to start something romantic with her for the first year and a half of school. We were constantly together—sometimes alone, and many times with our tight group of friends. She was the only girl. She was a good friend, but I knew she didn't see anything more there. But I foolishly persisted and became somewhat obsessed with the stupid quest.

I think she eventually figured out what I had been thinking for so long, and one night she invited me back to her place. She took pity on me. I remember it as a very bland experience. It wasn't at all how I had imagined it. And as I was looking back upon what had happened, a harrowing vision popped into my head. She was saying something softly in the middle of our embrace.

"What was it again? Was it a sigh of either feigned or real pleasure, or was it a hushed and barely audible 'no'?"

I couldn't remember for the life of me. I played the moment over and over and over again in my head.

"Did she want me to stop and I just kept going?"

The vision was would continue to haunt me long after that. She and I did maintain our friendship throughout the rest of college, and she was extremely supportive of me after my incident senior year. But I still couldn't grasp hold of that particular memory.

"I might very well be a despicable person," I thought to myself.

Then came the thoughts of my wild and drunken behavior throughout college. Turning over trashcans and sending them barreling down the stairs of the dormitory. Urinating all over campus, sometimes in the strangest of places. Shouting obscenities, menacingly confronting random people on the pong table, and generally making girls feel uncomfortable in my presence. I continued to question myself.

"What the hell was I thinking? And what kind of horrible things did I do that I don't even remember?"

Revisionist projections plagued my mind.

And as I began to think about all those terribly shameful memories and dark spots, I started to talk them out. It was time to finally be honest. I recounted my entire past, especially all of the wrong I had done.

All alone, I paced around my apartment and spoke clearly and aloud for anyone or anything to hear. I was sick of the blinders, the tunnel vision, the fragile ego, and all of the bullshit. I would bare myself completely and accept any and all consequences. It was time to take responsibility.

As the memories poured out, something else began to happen. I started to hear pounding on the walls. Sometimes it was only one bang. Other times it was a series of bangs.

"Is someone putting up pictures on the walls next door?" I wondered.

The pounding persisted, all night. And it wasn't just from one side, either, it was from all over—upstairs, downstairs, left and right.

And the pounding synced up perfectly with my words. It surely meant something. Based on the timing, I would soon figure out that one bang meant "*Yes*," two meant "*No*," and a series of pounding meant "*Definitely not*," or "*Stop talking*." Even though I heard many continuous stretches of pounding, I never let up on my chatter. It was one of the most important things I had ever done, and I couldn't stop there.

"But who's pounding? Who's trying to communicate with me? Is it my parents messaging me remotely? Is it my friends or classmates?"

I couldn't be sure, but I slowly began to understand this entity, whatever it was. When the pounding would come, how loud it would be, and how many bangs would be useful clues for my investigation.

A nuanced understanding of the phenomenon of the pounding soon expanded into a holistic knowledge of all of the creaks, beeps, buzzes, and other previously overlooked noises around me.

"Are there multiple entities? Can some of them see me through electronic lights, while others cannot?"

I covered the computer, the alarm clock, and the cable box for safety.

With my sleuthing capacity back in full force, I could once again sense the numbers and colors popping out at me. This time, though, my new amorphous netherworld would give birth to free-forming connections, sometimes between seemingly incongruous concepts.

Analogy, metaphor, and symbolism took center stage as I began to uncover groundbreaking links within philosophy, psychology, anthropology, and religion. Nothing was out of bounds. I would soak in more and more about my subtextual reality than ever before. And the answers were coming quickly.

"I understand the red and black of the world," I thought, "but what about the rest of the palette?

"Let's start with the basics. White vs. black: yin and yang, yes and no, truth and lies, purity and degradation. Grey makes up the shadows in between, the unknown, the uncertain. Also, cooler colors tend to complement warmer ones. The fire and the passion burning in man are offset by the cool and comforting care of woman. If men are from a certain red planet, then women must be from the blue one.

"And blue is the color of the water that helps to counteract the flame. If I ever meet a girl, she would certainly be blue in nature. But, although they have the fire, men also have some darkness in them. The red planet isn't really red after all, is it? No, it has shadows of black, so men are more of a maroon type."

This would be a marker of myself.

"And yellow are the rays of the sun, the glare of a light bulb, a golden aura. This is what it means to be enlightened and evolved. Surely my metaphysical knowledge, telepathy and subtextual experience fit into this category of thought.

"And if blue is the cool water, then green must be the steady Earth. No frills, no bells and whistles, just on-the-ground reality."

This would be the counterpart to higher-level enlightened thought. It would be static, normalized, and calm. No whispers, no thoughts, no talking, just hush. When I flew too high into the yellow light, I would often be directed back down to the green zone. Sometimes green was about being basic—so basic as to be thickheaded, or even somewhat stupid. Sometimes it would be a clear reprimand to stop thinking and postulating.

Next.

"Purple is the color of that children's show character which many claim to be a homosexual representation. Is that what this color means? No, it's simply purple passion—sexual desire of any kind. And the effeminate color is actually pink. This represents homosexuality. But if paired with blue, it's the femininity of woman. If paired with black, it's purely heterosexual, or 'not gay.' If paired with grey: 'maybe gay,' or bisexual."

More pairings.

"Red and white: true love, or love at first sight. Red and grey: a lack of certainty that love is real, maybe a confirmation that what we call love is really just the effects of many standard biochemical reactions in the brain.

"Blue and white: clean thoughts about women, non-sexual…maybe even homosexual…purity toward women. Blue and grey: lack of knowledge of my future with a potential mate. Blue and green: water and land, human beings living on Earth. Blue and red: both a relationship and love—the ultimate aspiration.

"Purple and white: unblemished passion for women, as opposed to the perverseness of black and purple. Purple and grey: the halfway-lascivious and most common male view of women. Purple and yellow: forbidden interplay of passion or sexuality and the gift. Purple and blue: healthy heterosexual passion."

Culture and geography.

"China is a Buddhist country, so it must be represented by yellow. Indians wear colorful saris, and most often the ones they wear in my apartment complex are orange. The Indian flag does have orange in it, right? Oh, but China's flag is red *and* yellow, so this must be communism.

"And many of the westernized, English-speaking countries inconspicuously have red, white and blue flags. Judeo-Christian principles maybe? I already know from previous experience that the red-and-black dichotomy is steeped in religion. But the Star of David is blue, and the flags of many Muslim countries have some green in them. So the red/black interplay must involve Christianity then.

"Brown: the skin color of African Americans. The melting pot of America—black, brown, white, yellow, and red people—let's just go with beige."

I would see the government here as well.

Now some application. Cars.

"White car with a left turn signal: '*No*'; right turn signal: '*Yes*.' Black car—just the opposite. Grey car with a right turn signal: '*Unsure*'; left turn signal: '*Yes*,' since it is not, not certain, therefore, it is certain."

Confusing sometimes, huh?

"Maroon car, right turn signal: '*You're right*'; left turn signal: '*You're wrong*' and/or '*Stop what you're doing/thinking.*'"

Signs, signs, everywhere I looked. "*One Way, Do Not Enter, Caution, Stop.*" And so on and so on.

Numbers, numbers, numbers. All those numbers. Let's start with the loneliest:

One: The self, the power of action, free will in practice. Also: The ultimate unity, what some may call God.

Two: The combination of two "ones," a heterosexual relationship, a peaceful togetherness. Simply put: Peace.

Three: Initially, the vulgarity of the middle finger, but soon translated into the concept of pain. Also, and sometimes confusingly: Homosexuality.

Four: A joining or togetherness of two peaceful counterparts, the concept of love.

Five: Irritation or frustration that doesn't quite translate into pain, but still worse than a mere annoyance. Also: Most whispering thoughts.

Six: The mark, evil, hatred.

Seven: Initially heaven, but later refined into the broader concept of religion.

Eight: Infinity, or concepts in time.

Nine: "On the cloud," happiness, elation.

Zero: Harmony, static baseline, lack of chatter or whispering.

Now on to higher numbers and combinations:

Ten: The commandments, generally accepted principles of productive societal behavior, a good way to treat each other.

Eleven: Two type A "ones" abutting each other, conflict, competition.

Twelve: From one person into two, finding a partner. Also: Making peace.

Thirteen: Initially, an individual's submission to Allah through suffering, Islam. Later: My travails through pain, me, a self-identification marker.

Fourteen: One person generating love. A generally prohibited or dismissed symbol.

Fifteen: Initially, a person succumbing to frustration. Later: The number of my shameful indiscretions at the time, prostitution.

Sixteen: One individual generating hatred. Rarely used.

Seventeen: An individual representation of religion, Jesus Christ.

Eighteen: Activities through time and space, time travel.

Nineteen: Making oneself happy, self-love. Usually pejorative in nature.

Twenty: The twentieth letter of the alphabet, "t," the cross, Christianity.

Twenty-three: Initially, the jersey number of a world-renowned sports figure, supreme talent, dominance with skill. Later: A heterosexual and homosexual coming together, a meeting of the minds between two competing factions, peace between unknown warring parties, a fine balance within the universe.

Twenty-four: Heterosexual relationship turning into love or marriage.

Twenty-five: The amount of cents in a quarter, "change," the ability to adapt for the better.

Twenty-seven: Peace among all religions, the ultimate societal aspiration, an end to mindless bloodshed and war.

Twenty-nine: Happiness within a heterosexual relationship. Also: Happiness with peace.

Thirty-five: The two numbers that correspond to the two opposite ends of the strands of DNA, human genetics, human nature, human beings.

Thirty-nine: Transitioning from a period of pain or depression into a happy state, turning the proverbial ship around. Also: Manic depression.

Forty-two: Divorce or breakup.

Forty-five: The last two digits of the year of the detonation of the first atomic bomb, an irreversible catastrophe, a scorched-earth policy decision, taking down the ship in spite or anger.

Forty-eight: An unending, cyclical, and infinite realm of love. Regarded as unattainable and generally dismissed or negated easily.

Seventy-six: The last two digits of the year of the signing of the Declaration of Independence, freedom, breaking away from the chains that bind, often the promise of finding a committed relationship to snap the shackles of loneliness.

Now, although these were the staples, other combinations and permutations often arose. Many times I tackled lists with more than two numbers. Backwards combinations often worked just as well.

Each letter of the alphabet corresponded to its sequential number in alphabetical order. Acronyms, words, initials, etc. could be decoded summarily. License plates of other cars on the road were the basis of much communication and knowledge gathering. Longer strings of characters like telephone numbers and addresses were also in play. Dates were important.

Most of this became second nature after a while. I wouldn't have to go through the process of thinking about a concept, matching up the symbols, and then extracting the meaning. I saw the world in code. In real time. It was a secret language, and I thought I might be one of the only ones in the world who could speak it. And I was fluent.

Then came the scratching. At first it was just an itch here or there. Then itches in the same spot over and over again. I began to realize that the communication was happening within my body as well. It was clear that the entity or entities had open access to my brain. They could pinpoint an area to stimulate, and then send the signal. Generally, an itch on the left side of my body, arm or leg would be a negative, and the right side a positive.

Fingers and toes. The right hand/foot was me, the left hand/foot the entity/entities. The symbolic numbers carried over to the fingers and toes. Either thumb/big toe: "*Good,*" "*OK,*" "*Acceptable,*" or desired result. Right hand—Index finger: friend. Middle finger: gay, also pain. Ring finger: platonic love. Pinky: my frustration. Left hand—Index finger: girlfriend. Middle finger: gay or pain for the entity/entities. Ring finger: marriage or romantic love; also the somewhat confusing concept of motherly love. Pinky: frustration for the entity/entities.

Face. Inside eye: "*I'm sorry.*" Outside eye: teardrop or sadness. Nose: close family, intimate relationship. Across the mustache area: "*It's a joke,*" "*Forget about it,*" or "*Disregard that.*" Chin cleft: respect. Corners of the mouth: happiness, laughter, or acceptance. Forehead: frustration. Temples: thinking, directive to think, or intelligent thought. Scratching the head: "*I don't know,*" unsure, unfamiliar, or unaware. Running the hand through the hair: sure, confident, correct, aware. Ear: listening, directive to listen, or understanding. Chin: "*Maybe.*" Eyebrow: anger. Stomach: "*Thank you,*" or gratitude. Cheeks: embarrassment. Between the nose and the eye: request, pleading, "*Please.*" Heart: love. Middle of the chest: me or myself. Wrists: exasperation, suicide. Back: "*Back up,*" "*Slow down,*" "*Stop thinking,*" "*Erase that last thought,*" or "*That last thought was wrong or misplaced.*" Lips: kiss, sexual passion. Under the front of the collar: desirous, "hot," sexually appealing.

Gesticulations. Hands together in a prayer motion: "*Please,*" polite request. Clasped fingers: two people "together," or in a relationship. Readjusting glasses: "*I see,*" "*I understand,*" or "*I'm paying attention.*" Arms crossed or intertwined: anger. Hands on hips: anger, frustration, or disappointment. Holding arms uncrossed: care, nurturing, compassion, transmission of good feeling.

Now, I knew that the entities had access to portions of my nervous system, most likely remotely.

But that then begged the question: "What else in my body do they have access to? Do they have control over my movement, my greater cognition, and my senses? Quite possibly."

I was learning more and more every minute of every day. I would take only one class and had no internship over the summer, so I would play golf with my parents here and there on the weekends and spend most of the rest of my time pacing around my apartment figuring things out.

One day I was staring at a map of the world and noticed something interesting. As I marked the locations of all the major ancient civilizations throughout history on the map, I began to connect the dots.

It was uncanny. All of these populated areas seemed to fit neatly along a continuous arc across the globe.

"This is big—really big," I thought to myself.

"And why do humans have such different physical characteristics anyway? Skin color, facial structure, height, body type? Is it possible that these societal groupings on Earth come from different origins rather than from a common ancestor? Is the world nothing but a petri dish for several different alien subcultures?"

The signals were fortuitous.

"Whatever it is, I'm on to something."

"Are the aliens an advanced race that has cracked the enigma of time travel? Is this what all the strife has been about? Have they set up these cultures, societies, and religions, only to go back in time and try to change things over and over again? Were the major religious figures throughout history planted at moments in time for a reason? Were they trying to correct the ills of society through time travel?"

"Or is this simply an experiment to see who makes it out alive, who wins, whose ideas are the best? Or better yet, is it all just a test to see if we can truly get along as a species, or if we will eventually eradicate ourselves due to our shortcomings and weaknesses? Are we worthy?”

CHAPTER SIX

I Surrender

OVER THE SUMMER COURSE I TOOK, the negatives started to creep in. I sat all the way in the back of a full classroom and tried intently to type every word the professor said. But he would get deep into his discussions and was constantly trying to motivate the students. He would keep the class wide awake by banging over and over again on the podium. I could see then that most of my thoughts about the material were clearly off base. But I endured.

As second-year classes neared, the whispering was in full force. All lines of communication were open, and innovative ideas about complex concepts were forming freely. But as classes started, I began to feel the wrath again. The whispers became louder and more intense.

"Is this my classmates speaking to me?" I wondered. "Does everyone know what's going on? Does everyone have this telepathic ability and I'm simply far behind the curve? Am I a remedial telepathic?"

Then came the "snap" negatives. At the mere inception of a negative thought, I would hear a reflexive whisper. The innocuous negative would transform instantly into the most extreme of negative thoughts or words about that particular concept.

Just seeing an African American would prompt a loud "N-word" thought. In fact, no races or ethnicities were immune. Although the mental harassment ran the gamut, the go-to debasement of myself would be "gay" or "pervert."

"I must have Tourette's of the damn mind." I thought.

There was no way to stop it or control it. I simply had to do everything I could do to contain it.

I was somewhat of a laughing stock—the guy who couldn't deal. I devised several techniques to keep the thoughts at bay. I would concoct mantras, such as "Holy Roller," to repeat over and over again in my head to cut off the unwanted thoughts. My goal every day of classes was to "pitch a shutout," meaning to disallow every negative thought that invaded my brain. Man, was I exhausted.

Then came the visuals. I would be at home trying to sleep. Unwanted images would pop up incessantly, keeping me awake at all hours of the night. Sometimes shapes, sometimes colors. And sometimes pictures or faces. Crystal clear photographs. Then moving images. Sometimes even pornographic videos. Sometimes things I had never seen before.

"How are they able to transmit these images into my brain?" I asked myself.

I did have some defense technology of my own, though. I could also create images in my head. I would "erase" their images and transplant some of my own. I would create parchments of their unwanted images, roll them up, and toss the scroll out to leave a blank black screen.

"This must be an exercise, a boot camp of sorts," I figured.

I was still learning, and I would get better.

But the fights continued. A tingling of the middle finger, the thought shout of “Gay!”, a pink three appearing up on the television screen. Sometimes all at the same time. The coincidences were astounding. After a while I began to understand that these were no mere coincidences after all.

“I mean, what is the probability that all these things happen at exactly the same time? Besides, it’s not just me, or the entities controlling my brain, who are emitting the signals. It’s my *environment*.”

The cars, the television, the street signs and billboards, the sounds in my apartment, other people talking. It was all synced. And the syncing became more and more refined over time.

As I would make the drives to and from my parents’ house in the suburbs, I would turn on the radio. The songs would coincide perfectly with my thoughts, the license plates, and the objects outside my car.

I thought I’d try something. I flipped through the radio stations quickly, just to hear a word here or there from each station. Even those few words were in sync.

“So what exactly is going on here?” I thought to myself. “Logically, this has to involve time travel of some sort. Obviously super-complex time travel. If the entities know where I’m going to be and at what time, they can produce the thoughts in my head or give me the body signals, and things can therefore sync up. They might be able to control activities on the outside as well. If they can get into my brain, then surely they can get into the brains of others and make them act or appear in certain places at certain times. But imagine the amount of time and energy involved in such a production. If this is all about me, then this is an enormous undertaking.”

I was overwhelmed…

Back at classes, the thought shouting got louder and more negative. No matter how hard I tried to fight through it, I couldn’t concentrate completely on the professors’ words. But I plugged away. I had techniques, and I could do all right in class if I didn't talk much. At home, reading the material was a little easier, and I could get through most of it.

But even then, the negativity was overwhelming. My apartment overlooked a parking lot across the street. The attendants would jam cars in bumper to bumper all day long. This was certainly no "easy out" parking lot.

And when they tried to move some of the cars, they would bump into the stationary ones, and their alarms would go off. All day long. Incessant honking, buzzing, beeping, and blaring sirens competed—successfully—for my attention. The noise was suffocating. And because they were continuous loud noises, they had to be negative in nature. I was being reprimanded nonstop.

Then the construction. The managers of the apartment complex decided to build out the fitness facility in my wing. The pounding. Oh, the pounding. I knew only one environment to study in. It was my safe zone. And now it was being invaded.

Saturated and spent, I was unable to continue with my studies. I had already dropped one class, I couldn't read the chalkboard from the back row of the classroom, and I couldn't understand a word the professor was saying through his thick accent. Not to mention all that commotion in my head. I had to get in touch with the doctor again.

When I went in to see him, I told him only what I thought was necessary. My knowledge was too important, and anyway, I was pretty sure he wouldn't get it. Plus, there was that black cloud of lockdown on the floor up above in the hospital looming over my head. I could not go back to that. I knew too much.

So I just told him that I was having racing thoughts again. I didn't delve too deep into it. The doctor asked me a plethora of questions, but I sidestepped all of them and was curt with all of my answers. He prescribed an oval yellow pill to replace the large round white one, to be taken with the other medication I was already on. I would take it as directed. I rested for a few weeks at my parents' house while the levels stabilized. The thoughts began to reel in a bit, but not without consequences.

I began to have trouble holding on to thoughts. I would make sense of something, only to be distracted by the next chain of reasoning. By the time I got to the third connection, the first one had been lost forever. I tried forcefully to search the recesses of my mind to retrieve the content, but it was useless.

Although I was interested in most of the material, some classes were harder for me than others. I spent much more time reading than I normally had to, because I would sometimes have to read sentences over and over again to grasp the meaning.

When I turned in my mock billable hours sheet to my legal writing professor, she seemed surprised. I didn't quite understand. It really did take me forty hours to write the entire contract. I was just being honest. In the end, though, a conscientious and gracious student who was assigned as my partner in that class helped me out. She carried me through our final project, so I was able to complete the coursework for that class and receive a good grade.

But one exam in particular threw me for a loop. Although it was a multiple-choice test, the professor required written explanation as well. I had only seen one exam like that before and was anything but confident with the format. But I thought I did well nevertheless.

When I got the results the next semester, I was shocked. I couldn't understand for the life of me how so many of my answers could have been wrong. All we read was a book of strict code, and I knew it backwards and forwards. This wasn't the typical malleable case law. So I thought I'd go in to the professor's office and try to negotiate my answers. I restudied much of the material and had my ammunition for the battle.

She summarily dispensed with all of my feeble arguments and was taken aback at my lack of understanding of the material. She asked, bewildered, how I was doing in my other classes. I could barely muster a soft “Well…” as tears filled my eyes.

The irony was that I had actually done very well in all my other classes—two good grades and two excellent ones. A few tears rolled down my cheeks uncontrollably, and I slunk out of the room, head down.

By the end of that year I had finally made a commitment to quit my dirty habit. My clothes stank up the closet, my breath smelled constantly, and it looked bad to boot. So one day I just stopped. Although I had been smoking for almost ten years at that point, the last ones very heavily, I knew all along that it was just a habit. I had also come to know, in many ways now, that the mind is much stronger than we often give it credit for.

And the drinking had stopped by then too. I had a beer on my birthday, and then a few on a day of symbolic hope, but I had been pretty dry for quite some time. Until the new year rolled around, that is.

A few days after an uneventful New Year’s Eve, I had become stir crazy and fed up with all the internal strife. I needed to get out and let loose. So I called the friend I had roomed with in the city two years before, and we went out to a local bar.

I ordered a vodka lemonade, and only a few minutes later, all that was left was a cup of ice. After a couple of hours, our whole table was littered with empty glasses. I think I counted eight in total. My friend had only had a few and clearly wasn’t too thrilled with the scene. He asked if I wanted a ride home, but I was on a roll and would head to the pool table. He asked several more times, but I continued to decline, telling him that a cab would be just fine.

The snowstorm was fierce and persistent, but I paid no attention. I had made a few friends on the pool table and was willing to continue the buzz. One of the girls agreed to come to another bar with me down the street. She convinced a couple of her friends as well. The only thing was that she had her car there, didn't drive much, and was afraid to drive in the thick powder.

No fear in me though. She gave me her keys, and wiper blades full blast, we trekked down the street in her SUV, doing about twenty-five. Thankfully, we got to the bar in one piece. More pool.

Then, as the night spilled over into early morning, it was finally time for them to head home. She was ready to leave, and it was pretty clear that I would not be going with her. Sadness crept in. I couldn't figure out why this always happened to me. It was so easy for most of my friends.

"What's wrong with me? Is it my looks? Is it the way I talk or act? I get along with most people. I can be charming. I always try to be polite and kind. Why not me?"

Then I remembered what had happened a few days before. My friend had asked me to pay for his vehicle delivery from another city. The driver only accepted cash, and my friend didn't have enough. I had helped him out that day, and he had paid me back in cash before we went to the bar. I now had money on me. A lot of money.

As I jumped into the cab, all options were on the table. I asked the driver for a fun place to go at that time in the morning. The first answer was the strip club down the road. I wavered. Then he asked me if I wanted to see a girl. I said yes, and he asked me for money. A few hundred-dollar bills in his pocket, he made some calls.

I arrived at the door of the shabby, rundown apartment building and knocked. A tired-looking woman with braided pigtails and a husky voice answered and let me in. She asked me for the cash, and I took everything I had in my pockets, including the spare change, and dropped it onto the kitchen table.

She watched the coins dance around on the Formica surface, turned her attention to me, called me cute, and went into the bathroom. I peeked into the other room and saw a woman asleep on the couch holding a small infant. After a while, the other woman came out of the bathroom and was ready.

What I did was risky behavior, and I knew it. But at that point there was no controlling it. Right in the middle, she popped up surprised, and said that she had to get something. She told me she would be right back and closed the front door behind her as she left the apartment. I waited for what seemed like forever, but it was probably only a few minutes.

Just then, something shook me up. I didn't know what, but I had to get out of there, immediately. I bolted out of the apartment and jumped down the stairs two or three at a time, hoping to get out of there and into my bed as quickly as humanly possible.

When I got out of the building, I could barely see five feet in front of me. The wind picked up and sheered my face. I clomped through several feet of snow, although not in any particular direction—just out of there. I figured I'd just have to make it to a major street and find a gas station or something. I had to keep moving.

Tears streaming, I couldn't stop asking why.

"Why is this happening to me? What did I do to deserve this?"

I had to get home. I walked down a few empty streets until I finally came upon an isolated diner. I sat down at the breakfast bar, caked in snow and tears, for the full restaurant of morning folk to see. After scarfing down some eggs and bacon, the lady behind the counter slipped me the bill. As I began to take the only credit card I had out of my wallet, she quickly turned back to me.

"Cash only."

I told the man sitting at the stool next to me that I was in a bad way, lost, broke, and without a ride. And I just needed to get home. He offered to pick up my check and give me a ride, and I had no choice but to accept. He probably didn't have the biggest paycheck, and he probably had to get to work very soon. I then knew without a doubt what it really means to be a human being.

Luckily, we got on the right road back to my parents' house, and about half an hour later I was home. I offered him money, anything to repay him for his generosity. He humbly declined, and I went in and went to bed.

I woke up ashamed. What had I been doing with my life over the previous five years? Things would have to change. Starting now. I would quit drinking completely. I would eat better. I would exercise and lose weight. And I would keep it in my pants.

Everything had come crashing down around me, but I still had one thing left—my will. So I would use it. But the whispering, banging, body signals, and synchronicity persisted. In fact, it got worse. Much worse. Although I was strong, the entities were also strong, and probably stronger. But I would battle it out, as I always had. Until one particular fight.

One day, I had already been frustrated, and I was bubbling up to the boiling point. I lashed out at the entities with my thoughts. They pushed back. In fact, I could feel them taking control of my body. My arm moved. Then my leg.

"Is this uncontrollable?" I wondered. "Which one of us actually did that?"

I fought back. I moved my arm, then my leg.

"Now who did that?!" I snapped at them.

Then I felt a tingling sensation around my neck.

"Are they trying to simulate a dog collar, or even worse, a noose?"

Then came the "flipping." The rationale I asserted for every concept I believed in would be turned around and thrown back in my face. I had had some deeply ingrained ideas, things that I had thought most of my life. They were part of my personality. Not anymore.

They flipped me on just about everything. My perspective was under attack by several other, more logical ones, with much more sound reasoning. I was no match for them. I tried futilely to draw a line in the sand, but in the end, it was no use. They had control of my brain, and there was nothing I could do about it.

I felt a sharp piercing pain in my head for a moment. Then some faint circus music. I knew what they were doing, but I was powerless. I would learn to fear that circus music.

As much as I detested the thought, I had to submit. I had to listen. I was being subjected to a highly intrusive and far-reaching investigation. I answered all of their pressing questions about me silently in my head. I tried to play keep-away between the somewhat benevolent ones and the more aggressive ones. Sometimes I would answer, keeping my thoughts quiet, but just by moving my eyes. I would never give up on two things though. They could take everything away from me, but not these: “God” and “Gay.”

I had never grown up as part of an organized religion. In fact, I scoffed derisively at most of it. It didn’t make logical sense to me. I didn’t believe all of the nonsense.

“A bearded white man up in the clouds watching us and judging our every move? Please.”

It was irrational and childish. It was an opiate for the masses. It was simply a source of comfort for those who were too scared to think for themselves. It was a power structure designed to subserviate. The universe was way too expansive to be limited to a God watching over our puny little Earth. I would not give up on this one. There was no way they could prove it to me or tell me otherwise.

“These entities might not be so smart after all,” I thought. “They certainly aren’t omniscient. In fact, they might even be human.”

And the shouts of “Gay!” held firm. But so did I. I had always liked women, and there was no doubt about that.

“Whatever it is—genetics, environment, or more likely a combination of both to some degree or another—I don’t have it.”

They shouted and shouted, and the constant references and insinuations were a nonstop blur. I was in the school cafeteria one day when I heard the thought shout a few times. Just then I noticed two women sitting across from each other talking a little louder than usual.

One of them said to the other something to the effect of: "Do you think he's gay?"

This hit me like a ton of bricks, but I wouldn't give up. I knew that I was right on this one. Even though the entities knew they could frustrate and anger me with this particular weapon, this battle would have to continue.

My days and nights melded together in a blasé yawn. I would study and go to classes, but I wouldn't go many other places. On the weekends, I would drive down the street to the video store to pick up some popcorn and a few movies to get me through the next couple of days. I would make my way to the drive-through window to get my medicine and drive back home. I would pick up the same lean lunch at the same store every day of the week, and I would eat my frozen lean dinners in front of the TV every night. I cut my calories almost in half.

I would run on the treadmill two or three times a week, but the endorphins certainly weren't pumping. If I were feeling particularly frisky, I'd walk across the street for a frozen smoothie treat. Highlight of my week.

I didn't talk to anyone, and they didn't talk to me. The signs were all nasty and vehement. I was to shut up every time I opened my mouth. I started to hear thought shouts of "CAN IT!" over and over again. So I stopped talking completely. I would offer only polite greetings and salutations. Direct questions would be answered in the affirmative or the negative and not much more. I was absent, a wallflower, a ghost.

But I still listened. I could see all the strange and crazy things going on around me and within me, but no one would know. I could see the discomfort in people's eyes.

"What's wrong with this dude?"

People were probably talking, but I couldn't concern myself with that. I just had to survive.

I studied hard, partly because I had to. Many of my classmates had already landed internships and had come through with their first-year grades. Many of them had chosen to wing the rest of their classes. But I studied harder than ever. It was all I had. Plus I probably needed to work twice as hard just to comprehend the material. I tried my best to simply keep to myself. Fortunately, though, I ended up doing pretty well in classes that semester.

But the run had taken its toll. I hadn't really smiled or laughed in as long as I could remember. I feigned it here and there, but I could tell that no one was buying. And I cried. A lot. Mornings before classes, afternoons at lunch, every trip in the car to and from my parents' place in the suburbs, and every night before bed.

The whispering was nonstop. Every minute of every day. It would become louder and clearer as I was entering or leaving consciousness, but it never stopped, and it was almost always negative. I was stuck, and I thought I might never get out.

Injury soon followed the insults. One night as I lay in bed, I felt a sharp pain in my rear end. The pain got progressively worse throughout the night. I tried to shift positions—on my back, on my side, in the fetal position. The pain persisted. It kept me up all night. And the next night.

It wasn't until after the weekend that I could see the doctor, and then the next day a specialist. The pain from the fissure was no match for the large needle though. In it came, time and time again. Over and over. Loud shouts of profanity echoed throughout the room and reverberated through the halls.

My bum still tender from the procedure, my mother gave me a round pink inflatable donut to sit on throughout the day. I needed it, and I brought it to class every day. As I still wasn't talking, no one could have known why the guy in the back row was always sitting on an inflatable pink rubber tube. But such are things, and I had more important issues to deal with.

Soon I had another final take-home exam to write. I plugged along, using notes and research, and this time I would have to present my analysis of alternative conflict resolution. As I dug into my analysis, the car alarms across the street began to blare. I would have to erase the previous sentence. It went on like this throughout the entire paper, but I eventually made it through some thirty pages.

After I healed up, I got a call from the friend who I had roomed with in the city a few years before, and he offered to take me out with a couple of his other friends. Having sworn off drinking, I offered to drive. They had fun and mingled while I leaned on the bar and stared off into space. I noticed a man at the end of the bar who looked exactly like a friend of mine from college.

"There's definitely something to this," I thought.

The resemblance, along with many other signs, occupied most of my attention throughout the night.

On our ride home, I was silent, as I had been the whole night. My friend's friend, who had had several drinks, made a particularly rude comment about my behavior. Without hesitation, my friend shot it down and thanked me for the ride. At least that was something nice to hear.

Then one night over the summer, a smoking buddy of mine who I hadn't seen in a while called me and asked if I wanted to see the neighborhood fair that was going on in the parking lot outside our apartment complex. I jumped at the chance to get out of the apartment, and we headed out to the street together. I had seen them setting up the sound systems from my window the day before. It reminded me of a similar thing I saw out of the hospital window in college.

"Is this all for me again?" I asked myself.

We strolled around a bit after visiting the fair. The streets were calm and quiet. Thoughts crept in as always, but things around me were syncing up and clicking pretty quickly. Actually, that managed to take a little of the edge off.

And soon I would be brought back to visions of a mushroom trip I had been on with some friends from college. Things were strange, but somehow also in place. There was an eerie sense of significance to everything. We eventually came upon a warehouse. The door was wide open, and we wandered inside. We traversed around some school desks, chairs, and other equipment. Memories poured in. I was sure we were there for a reason.

"Is all of this happening because of drugs I did in college?" I wondered. "Pot, mushrooms, ecstasy? They can create hallucinations, euphoria, and strange thinking, right? Maybe some of the drugs are still in my system, left in my spine or something. Or maybe the entities are intentionally conjuring up old memories to cause me to experience those sensations again, just in a different environment."

As the summer drew on, the signs persisted in directing me to stop thinking. So I learned to cut off my train of thought. Things would pop up, and I would shut them down. It wasn't always possible, but I could soon sense the firewalls forming within the pathways of my brain.

I eventually had to take a back seat. All of the free will I had been championing for so long had come to a screeching halt. No more type A personality, no more fire in the belly, and no more driving the car. I would simply listen and do as I was told. I was told not to write anything down—no grocery lists, none of my prized checklists, and especially no numbers. I was even slapped down every time I tried to do math in my head. So no more of that. Everything and anything that didn't absolutely require an executive decision, particularly for safety, was directed by the whispering. I was to go with the flow.

This was not an easy prospect. You go through your whole life doing things your way. You create your successes, and they are all yours. Sometimes you make mistakes, but many times they are the fault of others. You fight through adversity and make your own luck. You are free, an individual, a director of your own film. You control your own destiny. Not anymore.

So I submitted, hanging on to a small fraying thread of autonomy for emergencies and quick decisions only. It was painful at first, but I started to see more and more. Not just connections and synchronicities, but how the world worked. And more importantly, how *people* worked.

I began to look and listen. Not just to actions, but to ways of being. I began to notice how people approached one other and how they behaved around each other. I studied people and their psychological constructs. I had never noticed most of these nuances and subtleties of life before. It was fascinating. And the entities knew a hell of a lot about it. They were right a lot. It was frustrating, but this is why I continued to listen to them.

I'm not sure how much my parents knew about what was going on. But I knew that they certainly didn't know how deep this actually went, because I told them little to nothing. Over the summer, I continued to play golf with them, going through all the old motions.

One day, having nothing to do, I sat on the edge of my bed staring off into space and shutting thoughts down. My mother walked in and asked me what was going on. I told her that I was just quietly thinking to myself. She must have thought that that was kind of weird, but then again, weird is relative. It could have been worse, and I felt that I was doing pretty well at hiding my knowledge of the secret code.

I don't think my father knew as much. But as I said less and less, I noticed that something else began to happen. I would hear more directives from my parents. I was often being told to do this or that, and it seemed constant. I would simply oblige and carry on. But just as taking a back seat to the entities bruised my pride, this took a shot at my ego as well.

One afternoon in particular, my father was telling me how to connect a cable to the computer. I knew very well that I had superior knowledge of computers, but I held back. I just followed directions. I was sure I had a much better, faster way to do it, but I just let it happen. I felt a helpless pit in the middle of my stomach—a wound that was being pressured. But, once again, I said nothing and endured.

Another day on the golf course, I was sitting in the cart while my father was on the tee box. During my discovery phase, I had been thinking about political ideologies, in particular the societal advantages built into the theory of communism. Just as one of these thoughts popped into my head, I heard my father's voice loud and clear.

"Get it out of communism!!" he shouted.

But the strangest thing is that I'm not sure his lips were moving, at least not to form that sentence. It was a blur. I think he might have been kind of talking over himself at one point. And for sure no one on the golf course was talking about communism.

The source of the whispering began to shift from the entities to my family. My mother would be putting the silverware away, and the banging of the metal would be her telling me to shut up. My father would leave the cupboards open to tell me to "come out," presumably out of the closet.

On another occasion after golf, I was in my room just staring at the wood floor. I could see the number "3" etched into the wood with a circle around it. It wasn't really carved in, but if you looked very closely, you could barely make it out.

"Is this the sign for a birdie on a par four, or is it something trying to tell me that I'm gay? Or is it that I will be in pain forever?"

Another day, my brother and some other family members were over at my parents' place with us for dinner. He looked down at his cooked lamb, and I'm pretty sure I heard him mention that it was a poor, tortured animal.

"No doubt this is me he's talking about," I thought to myself.

I went into my room and stared at the huge flag that graced my wall. I just stood there, unflinching, for several minutes. At this point, I'm not sure whom I was communicating with, but I was pretty sure that the government was involved somehow. I was demonstrating to them that what I was going through was slavery, and they knew it.

Surprisingly, the thoughts and the whispering slackened a bit at that moment. They didn't want me to go down that path, but they chose not to reprimand me nevertheless. It was almost as if they feared that subject.

The course I took over the summer was an early one. Every morning I'd get up at the crack of dawn, start studying for class, and head down to the coffee shop right when it opened. I'd get my croissant and coffee to go, but every time before I'd leave, I'd be hit with an earful of the banging coffee tin. Damn that was loud.

To lighten the load of my next semester, I decided to take an extra course toward the end of the summer before the regular term started. It would only be a two-week class, but it was billed as "highly intensive." The reading was voluminous and the lectures long.

I spent all day and all night on that course. It must have taken me four hours to go through one of the technical patent cases. But, although it would soon all seem like nothing but gobbledygook, I still needed to get it right. So I turned off the TV and insulated myself from every external stimulus that I could shut out for those two weeks.

During class, I would feverishly type every word the professor said, although much of it was just general discussion. At a break in the class, she sneaked a peek at my computer screen, probably to see if I was paying attention. I'm guessing she did this because I would often stare into the distance trying to ward off intruding thoughts. The next day she asked me gingerly how I was doing. I said "OK," but I could tell very well that the strange behavior was more than apparent to everyone in the class.

The next day I was doing laundry in the basement and was thinking about some old concepts. I started to question the badge of red that I had so proudly worn during my first dive into the abyss.

"What is 'love' anyway? It's just an emotion, a construct we've developed to maintain stable and lasting relationships. It's a strong emotion, but that's all it is. We've been fooling ourselves. Life is not about some amorphous romanticized concept."

Then the orange saris came to mind. The Indian women in the building who wore them were almost always pushing infants in strollers. I think there were several young male Indian graduate students in the building who had brought their young families there as well.

"This is important," I told myself. "This is family."

My previously impenetrable red light was fading, and a new orange element had been born.

The next day in class, the professor had set out some materials in the classroom for the students to take a look at, maps or something. It was something to do with one of the cases, but something fun that the students were excited about. Many of the students got out of their seats to take a look, while I remained seated awaiting the next batch of notes.

After everyone returned to their seats, the professor asked the class what they thought. One student, very sharp and witty with most of his answers, took a shot. He said something pretty much word for word: "It looks like they've just replaced the red color with orange."

I nearly shit my pants.

Exhausted, I finished the course out strong. But I was once again approaching the saturation point. The whispering was unstoppable and continuous, and I had reached my limit. I would take walks around the apartment complex to clear my head. It was no help.

One night, as the tears streamed down my face, I asked the entities for help.

Over and over again, the only response was: "Help yourself."

Another whisper came, derisive and condescending, "You're never going to figure it out."

I couldn't take it any longer.

"How many sleeping pills will it take?" I asked myself. "What if I wake up? Will it destroy my insides and ruin my life if I don't get the job done? What about other ways? It could be done."

I suddenly felt a strange sense of calm wash over me. It was as if I were sensing two emotions, two selves at the same time—one dejected, lost, and hurt, and one at peace. The tears continued to stream.

Just then my father called. Sobbing uncontrollably, I debated for a moment whether to answer the phone, but I went ahead and did it anyway.

He asked if I was OK, and all I could muster through the tears was, "No."

Time to see the doctor again.

Although I was still pretty clammed up, the doctor took the initiative and decided to make some changes. He upped the dosage of the oval yellow pill and adjusted some of the other medication.

Looking back, I can see how hard it must have been for him to ad lib with so little information. He and my parents suggested that I also find a therapist who could help me work through some of my problems. The entities were strangely silent on the possible benefits of this decision, but I decided to contact a gentleman from a referral through my brother nevertheless.

He seemed kind and responsive, so we agreed to begin sessions of talk therapy. I wasn't talking very much at all at first, so I just continued to answer questions here and there with simple responses. The whispering and signals would dominate the discussions, but just having the sessions forced me to communicate with another person, and that would help.

Meanwhile, the higher doses of the medication soon took effect, and the thoughts did stabilize a tad. But that came with a familiar cost. My cognitive functioning and intellectual awareness took a pretty decent hit right away.

One morning, I was getting ready for breakfast and looked down to see orange juice in my cereal.

"Fantastic."

And the sexual side effects were alarming to say the least. But I was too embarrassed to bring this issue up with anyone, so it would go unaddressed for quite some time.

Again: "Just deal with it."

Although the tears continued to flow on every car ride to and from my parents' house, the sensation wasn't the same anymore. I hadn't had real raw emotion since before the first incident in college. But there was something even stranger going on this time. There was a sense of stasis or zeroing out, but the whispering and the thoughts kept coming.

I didn't feel sad per se. I mean, I was completely wrecked, devastated, and battered. Intellectually I was a mess, and I knew that. But there wasn't a deep, low *feeling*. In fact, there was no real feeling at all. So it was strange to cry like that. It was as if someone or something were crying for me—almost manual tears. And it showed no signs of stopping.

Back at school, there was actually kind of an upside amidst all the madness. The course load was much more manageable, and classes became more interesting. The directives still kept coming during class, so for some courses I eventually just stopped taking notes completely.

But this wasn't such a bad thing after all. It's amazing what can happen when you take a deep breath and just *listen*. No intensity, no feverish activity, just attentiveness and concentration. Over the next two semesters, I began to understand the lectures much better. Although I was watching from the back seat, I could still see the road. I was following the thoughts that were presented to me. It took much less out of me.

I took great interest in a few of my courses. One in particular had fascinating reading material and engaging lectures from an incredibly intelligent professor. I could see that it struck her as strange when the whole class went out for treats in the hall, while I sat alone with her in the class quietly reading.

But I enjoyed the class nevertheless. Not to mention that we could choose to write a take-home exam instead of a timed essay. I had been monitoring my sleep schedule and turning in early at night, so I got this one done with plenty of time to spare. No more all-nighters for me. And I wouldn't need them.

Although the class size was small, I received the award for the top take-home paper in the class. It was the first time in years that I felt some semblance of affirmation for anything I was doing. And it felt good.

One of the other classes I took that semester was particularly interactive. We were to present arguments for full-length mock trials in actual courtrooms. It was one of my favorite classes at the school. Opening statements to the jury, direct and cross-examinations, objections, closing arguments, and rebuttals were all required activities.

I was forced to express myself, and that was a good thing. Actually, I had to participate in the class to pass, so although the whispering persisted somewhat, I had to overrule much of the negativity and reprimands. And I did well. I was good at it. The nerves would kick in, but in a good way. It was an extension of the oral argument preparation that I had had in my first-year legal-writing course. I was still learning.

But, although I was performing in public speaking, these were still mostly scripted activities. I would think, plan, write, and memorize much of the material at home. I had to be on my toes here and there, but little was left to chance. And my social interaction with others was still super high on the scale of awkward and uncomfortable.

Actually, it had gotten really bad over the previous year and a half. So bad that I had lost almost all of my mojo. Social graces, witty banter, spontaneous charm—I used to have a decent amount of that here and there, or at least so I thought. But all of that was out the window by then. I had forgotten how to be a person around people. I had been shut in for so long that I couldn't relate anymore.

After finals were over, I was able to make it to the next family vacation at the familiar islands this time. My brother and his girlfriend were there along with my parents and myself. They had big news. At an elegant restaurant overlooking an exquisitely manicured garden, they told us of their engagement. They raised their champagne glasses and I my water, but I was still conspicuously absent.

One day while we were there, I went out onto the balcony outside my room and rested my arms on the railing. I began to ponder. As I looked down at the exotic flowers that graced the garden below, playful birds of all colors and sizes chirped away and flitted all over—across the garden, onto the balcony beside me, through the air effortlessly.

I thought about the directives, the lack of control, and the oppressive thoughts. "Is this what the rest of my life is going to be like?" I asked myself. "Depressed and downtrodden, an outcast, a stranger, a robot, a ghost? Or am I going to do something about it?"

Finally, an executive decision of consequence.

"I will talk again. I will wrestle myself out of this quicksand and find solid ground. Life is way too short. I will talk again.

CHAPTER SEVEN

Out of the Darkness

ALMOST IMMEDIATELY AFTER I ASSERTED my will again through speech, the whispering took a hit. I could feel it subsiding as I began to communicate. My conscious thought finally became my own again, if only for a few brief moments here and there. In any case, it certainly was a start.

On to the last semester of law school. It was still hard to find classmates to talk to. Most of the people I already knew were probably familiar with my behavior, and my social wounds were still too deep to strike up conversations with the folks in my new classes. So although I was learning to "be" again, I knew that I would be taking the long road back.

I took two classes pass/fail, so the pressure of making my grades was a little less intense than in previous semesters. But even after three finals were in the books, I still had my seminar paper to turn in.

Way behind, I had to make up some ground quickly. In the end, the core concept of my piece had to take a drastic turn into new and uncharted territory. But somehow I was able to roll through it and get it in on time. It was finally over.

As I gladly dotted the last period on my law school career, I found my way to a popular restaurant row in the city. A crystal-clear sunny day, and I was free. I ducked into a semi-fancy joint, and the hostess seated me alone at a table for four. I indulged—a king's feast, complete with a fruity electric-blue vodka drink.

As the waitress cleared the spread of empty plates and plopped an enormous chocolate dessert down on the table, she exclaimed jubilantly, "Now that's how it's done!"

The vodka put my stomach in a little bind as I hadn't had alcohol in ages, and I left the restaurant for the street painfully solo again. But I smiled at a minor victory, knowing that I wasn't about to push the envelope that day. The bar exam would be coming up soon, and I had to get ready for prep classes.

As I dropped the huge box of books down on the futon in my apartment, I had no idea what to expect. I unpacked. Some fill-in review books, some mini-reviews, and many, many larger-than-life full-text volumes.

"Shit," I thought. "What have I gotten myself into here?"

And it was no consolation whatsoever when I saw the suggested schedule of reading, class sessions, and practice questions. Ten- to twelve-hour days, seven days a week, two months straight.

"OK, so be it," I told myself. "Let's dive in."

As always, my studio apartment was my comfort zone and study lair. I opened the monstrous outlines with the fine print and got cracking. Car alarms. Ambulances. Pounding hammers.

"Two months?! This is going to be impossible."

I finally caved and hit the library. My productivity was slashed at least in half.

"OK, let's just deal with the noise pollution at home then and try to keep the mind off the symbolic relevance and the whispering."

I settled into prep classes and finally found out that reading the gigantic outlines page by page was probably not the best way to go. I adjusted and allotted more time to the practice questions, the class notes, and the review books, using the monster books only for reference. Having cut out a lot of fat, I was pretty much on track. But I still had to make it to the wedding…

I landed in the small-town airport with two big suitcases and one carry-on for a three-day trip. The limo pulled up to the country cottage, and we got out to meet the host. Barefoot and very pregnant, she showed me up to a room on the second floor where I would be staying with my cousin. I nearly busted my back dragging the suitcases up the stairs.

She asked me, smiling, "What, are you moving in?"

Little did she know how much law I had in that baggage.

Later that night, caviar and chilled vodka graced the restaurant patio as family and friends jovially mingled around before the rehearsal dinner. It was somewhat easier to interact with family there, but the comfort level was unsurprisingly pretty low. Wound up and still battered and bruised, I tried to feign a smile here and there. But I think most of my family and my sister-in-law's family and friends had already sensed that something was a little off, if not specifically at that time, then most probably in previous interactions. I figured I'd just have to make do.

The next day, I was summoned to a room upstairs at the house where the wedding would take place. I was asked, along with my sister-in-law's brother, an attorney, to serve as a matrimonial witness. I was having trouble concentrating with all the hustle and bustle of the pre-ceremony arrangements. Ample laughter and clinking wine glasses, festivities were afoot. But I just sat there, trying to hang on to every word of the document. People were probably wondering why I was deconstructing and analyzing a fairly straightforward testimonial. But I was determined to fully understand the meaning of the text, and I eventually got pen to paper.

After the ceremony, I stood off to the side while the party ramped up. One of the bridesmaids approached me and asked if it felt weird that my brother was getting married. Weird feeling yes. But not an emotion. And not about my brother's wedding. I could see that it was a great day for him and everyone around him—I could grasp that. And it was nice to see. But in the end, I wasn't really there. It was clear to me that the world I was living in was foreign to everyone else's. They could share a common perspective, while mine was solitary.

But I tried to manufacture a smile and flushed the two glasses of wine out of my system with a copious amount of water. I couldn't afford to be hung over—I only had a few days for all of Real Property, and I had to make them count.

I quietly looked on as dance party broke out poolside and boisterous partiers tossed each other into the pool fully clothed. A strange sense of calm washed over me. Not really a peaceful one, though—a more detached feeling, as if I were watching from far, far away and not really experiencing. I had no real sense of who I was or what I was doing.

I got home with a daunting catch-up session shouting at me from the pages of the schedule. So I plugged away. But as the course wound down, I found that I'd be a little short on time and would have to skim over a few of the concepts. For that, I'd go to the review books.

"Oh man, if I had only known that before!"

These two books had everything in them, concise and to the point. Packed with helpful hints, tips, and study suggestions, these outlines were definitely the way to go. So I just crammed with them for the last few days and hoped for the best.

Two days, twelve hours. The noise signals kept popping at me during the exam, and I tried to squeeze them out the best way I knew how. I got on a roll during the second session of multiple-choice questions and felt pretty strong. Until the essay portion, that is. I remember one in particular. It was one of the topics I had had to skim, and I felt pretty lost. So I just used the facts, added a dash of law here and there, and drew out the argument as long as I could to make it look like a real answer.

In between sessions, I went outside for lunch. Many people were fretting nervously trying to get some last-minute memorization in. I vowed to stay even-keeled and just let things happen. As I looked over, I saw a woman sitting cross-legged on a short stone ledge abutting a garden. Her eyes were closed and she held her hands in a familiar-looking meditative pose.

"Must be Buddhist or something," I thought.

Back in the testing facility, the last session was tough, but I slogged through.

"Pencils down."

My sense was that it would be totally hit or miss—I figured that I was probably somewhere on the edge of passing. As I made my way out of the building, I turned to walk back through the courtyard to find a cab. When I approached the open square, I came upon a group of folks in colorful robes.

"You've got to be kidding me."

A gaggle of Buddhist monks was wandering around, heads fully shaven, wearing flowing maroon garb with yellow sashes.

"That just happened."

The professional responsibility portion of the bar exam was much shorter, much more manageable, and all multiple choice. So that worked out nicely. I played the waiting game for a while, and the results from the big test finally came in. I'm pretty sure that the skin of my teeth was a just few points, but I'm not positive. No point totals. If I remember correctly from the breakdown, my average positions relative to the other test takers over the various concepts weren't that great. But to the system that didn't matter: I was now a lawyer.

Thoroughly spent, I reserved some time for a deep breath and some golf. One day, as I sat in front of the large windows in my parents' living room staring out onto my mother's sunlit garden below, my father approached me. He had been asking me how I wanted to proceed with my career, and I hadn't had any good answers—for him or for myself. So he broached an interesting topic.

"Why don't you come work with me?" he said.

He mentioned the possibility of some astounding numbers in the future, over the next ten years or so.

"Ten years?!" I thought. "Yeah right. How can I commit to ten years at this point? I don't even know if I'll get through tomorrow."

So I told him I'd have to think about it.

By that time, the extended lease for my apartment in the city had run out, so it was time to pack up. Having been idle for a little over a month, I had gotten to thinking. And with the thinking came more symbols and body signals. As my mother helped me wrap up the plates, bowls, and glasses in my apartment, numbers and colors jumped out of their familiar hiding spots. I acquiesced to doing a little investigative work, but it soon turned sour. I walked downstairs to get a dolly, scalp itching incessantly. I didn't know much of anything, and I was being reminded of that.

Sweaty and frustrated, I slunk into the passenger seat en route to my old bedroom at my parents' place. We stacked my few possessions, mostly books, into one of the unused garage spaces at the house, and I settled in again. I wasn't planning on an extended stay by any means, but I knew that I had to get my bearings back.

During my stay there, I got a notice for a ten-year reunion party for my high school. I debated for a while, but in the end I decided that it might be good for me to get out and see people again. So I hopped in the car and drove downtown.

Many familiar faces zipped around recounting old stories and catching up on new ones. I was still pretty zonked out and wandered around for a bit. I said a few hellos here and there, but I basically just weaved aimlessly through the crowd. I made a firm stand not to use the social lubricant there as well, especially with the car keys on me. By that time I had learned my lesson, and I wasn't about to loosen the reins that night.

After a few laps around the banquet room, I bumped into the girl I had dated briefly after senior year. As if things weren't awkward enough. We chatted for a while, although I didn't have much of anything to say—certainly nothing witty or charming. I was unemployed, broke, and living with my parents. Stellar combo for a reunion conversation.

But she graciously allowed me to tag along and share her table. I let out a quiet sigh of relief, knowing that I wouldn't have to pace around by myself anymore. After some minimal conversation at the cocktail table, we took a brief stroll outside by the river. It was a pleasant night, and we walked mostly in silence. When we got back to the table, some of our other old classmates came by to chat.

As I had been hermitting myself for quite a while by then, I missed all of the nuances, and actually many of the main points, of the more sophisticated conversations about politics and current events. In fact, I'm pretty sure I didn't even know where I stood on many of the issues.

Part of it was that I just wasn't that well informed, but the other part of it was that I hadn't really even developed a worldview yet. I had been shut in, both mentally and physically, for so long that I hadn't had a chance to experience common reality as an adult. So I just listened to their conversations, mostly in silence, interjecting awkwardly here and there.

I soon found myself standing with a group of old friends that who had been in the honors track with me in school. It was good to see them, but I still didn't have much to say. Some of them had gone on to have exciting careers, had been to interesting places, and had met fascinating people. I was silent.

One of my friends mentioned to me caringly that it looked like I had "mellowed" a lot since high school. Yup, that punkish high school kid of way back when was definitely not present that day. He hadn't been around for a while.

Back at my parents' house, I got a call from the drinking buddy I used to go to the pool hall and the bars with. He was one of the only people in town I had hung out with regularly, and again, I needed to get out of the house. So he drove, and we went out to a few places. The pool hall had shut down by then, and the other neighborhood bars had become old news as well. So we went to a restaurant down the street to have a few glasses of wine.

We soon got to talking about the old high school group. After the first few sips, the wine began to go down easier. But more importantly, the words started to come—and quickly at that.

I told him that what he had been through with the other kids was not his fault and that much of what they were doing was tearing him down just to make themselves feel better. I also said that it was not his, but rather their, insecurities and unresolved issues which had been driving their actions. I went on to say that he should never blame himself for the undeserved suffering that others had inflicted upon him.

After I finished speaking, he smiled and said, "Wow, you could do this for a living."

I had never really been able to communicate on a level like that before. Not even before the whole mess started. Something was desperately trying to emanate from deep within me. It had been tamped down for so long, and now it was finally time to see what was inside.

My friend had always enjoyed playing the guitar and had aspirations of being a big-time musician someday. He figured he'd get his start by playing some open mics in the city and testing the waters. So I decided to go to downtown with him now and then to a few spots in a hip, artsy area of the city. We'd have a few drinks and catch a few football games on the bar TVs, and I saw him play once or twice.

But, although things had begun to look up for me a little bit by then, we still didn't have a whole lot to talk about. My thrills involved deep investigation of sophisticated issues, and he embraced a more light-hearted approach to life. He would soon move to another city, though, and I would have a big decision to make.

By that time, I had been out of school for several months and was certainly not about to go internet searching for another internship position again. And I figured that working with my father might prevent a nightmare boss scenario. I would have some flexibility with my work schedule, and I'd be coming into the industry already basically at the top. But most importantly, I'd have real job. So I said yes.

My father had been with his financial services firm for almost a quarter-century by that time, but he had begun to have misgivings about staying there. He had a plan in the works to transition to a different firm but wasn't completely sold on the idea just yet.

So we decided to see how it would go if I started out first with the firm he was still working with. That way, I could gain some experience in the industry while he thought more about a potential move. I soon began the application process, but as that process became more and more onerous, my father's patience began to thin. The grievance list was mounting, and the pile would eventually topple over.

So he reached out to some other firms, and the negotiations began. He enlisted the help of a securities lawyer to help us out with the provisions of the proposed contracts and for guidance throughout the process. He wanted me to be the point person for communication with the lawyers and the other firms. I didn't have a day of real legal work experience in my life, nor had I ever worked in finance or with corporate bigwigs. In fact, I had never really been employed at all. But like it or not, I now had a seat at the big boys' table.

However, if I were to be a real professional, I would have to have a place to live in on my own. I would certainly not be wheeling and dealing from my old high school bedroom at my parents' house.

So I went and found a listing for an apartment in an iconic building in the city. The units there had been some of the most luxurious and sought-after condos in the city for many, many years. Although it was by then an older building, it was still well known, and the location was prime. And the views of the lake were astounding to say the least. You could even see the fireworks below during the summer nights. I was definitely sold.

But I soon found out that the negotiation thing isn't always that easy. The woman who owned the unit in the listing seemed to like me, but likeability wasn't enough. I had no steady income, no real assets to speak of, and no substantive employment history. Good luck with that. I was far too proud at first to ask for my father's help, and even when I did find out that he could co-sign the lease, by then it was too late. She was scared off.

My parents then suggested that I try to purchase a place, with their help of course. They figured that I would soon have income to pay the mortgage, and that I would be able to build equity in the home over the long term. Not to mention that the real estate could serve as a good investment for my future. So I went hunting. I selected four different agents to get maximum exposure to the market, and we looked at unit after unit.

"A lot of space and light, a great view, washer and dryer in-unit, granite countertops, wood floors, a dazzling lobby"—blah, blah, blah.

The best of everything would come at a cost. And I just couldn't find the perfect place. Nice, clean apartments with great setups of modern furniture and art seemed rather appealing, while the ones with all the amenities but dirty clothes hanging out of the hamper didn't. It was hard for me to grasp that I was buying the space and not the owner's stuff.

Eventually, I came up with a short list of about four units, all at different spots around the city. I asked my mother to come downtown and help me select the best one. She liked a couple of them but thought that we could do better.

After the last showing, we saw the agent off and walked toward the lake. Along the way, we came upon an advertisement for a new construction and strolled in. We chatted for a while with the salespeople and looked at some pictures and prices. Then came the presentation.

An older gentleman, probably in his eighties, flashed his laser pointer all over models of the city and a future representation of the building we were looking at. It was actually kind of riveting. And, although we were going in blind, seeing as though the building was only about a quarter finished, it seemed like the best option. We would have to discuss further.

Meanwhile, negotiations with the firms took off. Clandestine meetings at the home involved tea, cake, and passionate presentations—both by my father about his business model, and by the representatives of the firms about what they were prepared to offer us. Four firms, and they all had different approaches. One dropped off fairly quickly, leaving three solid offers.

Although my father's compensation was pretty much ballpark with all three, my projected compensation varied—one mediocre starting salary, one pretty good, and one the big bucks. Funny enough, although my pay would be peanuts within the scope of the larger deal, this particular provision had considerable sway with my father. He would see how they treated me, and this would affect him. After all, his master plan was to eventually leave his business to me after he retired. And I was his son.

The big-bucks deal also had the shortest contract, and my father liked that, so we delved deeper into that offer. Throughout the negotiations, I tried my best to concentrate. I would keep quiet most of the time so as to hide my novistry, but I felt compelled to participate now and then. I was being billed as the big-shot intellectual lawyer, and I had to play the part.

My concentration would wax and wane, and some symbols, whispering, and distractions sidetracked me here and there. They weren't easy to push out, to say the least. And after one meeting in particular, the manager even asked my father if I had been paying attention to their conversation.

I had been staring down at my coffee mug trying to latch onto every word, all the while trying to ward off unwelcome thoughts. So, although it must have looked as if I were spacing out, I was really focusing as intently on their discussion as possible. But I certainly wasn't getting everything.

What I knew I could tackle, though, was the written communication. That didn't require any interaction, and the clock would be on my side. So I took care of refining, polishing, and even inserting content into many of the letters, emails, and written presentations to the firms. I also understood most of the lawyer's writing, and I could run through many of the contractual issues with him. Even with the whispering, I could help make some sense of that.

Near the end of the negotiations, the big-bucks firm flew us out to their headquarters to do the rounds and to meet "important" people. Unsurprisingly, they put us up in one of the most extravagant hotels in the expansive city. I placed the key card into the door of the hotel room and opened it.

"Holy shit!"

This room was probably three times the size of my apartment in law school. It had two freaking bathrooms, a living room, and a dining room. Champagne, strawberries, and a cheese plate were awaiting me to boot. My father's room was half the size. Either they messed up the names, or they knew damn well how to negotiate.

We went to several meetings with the bigwigs, but not much out of me. Toward the end of our scheduled visit, we ended up in an enormous office with a picture window overlooking the entire city.

In came the big boss. I just sat there on the couch while this man, noticeably calm and genteel, tossed some softballs to my father. I had a little trouble with directing my attention, though. My gaze was too intense sometimes, and I didn't want to appear strange. So I'd take a break now and then to catch a glimpse of the sun pouring in through the huge picture window. And I said almost nothing.

After some complimentary deli sandwiches from my father's favorite shop, we hopped into the limo and headed toward the airport. We arrived home to a monstrous wheel of cheesecake—one of my favorite treats. It had been waiting for us in the fridge.

We didn't know at first where it had come from, but we would soon figure it out. I had mentioned to the manager in negotiations that I had liked that particular deli's cheesecake, and the wheel just happened to be from the very same deli in the city we had just been to. It was a good touch, though a little overdone.

And after all that, some of the promises seemed too good to be true. My father just didn't trust the deal in the end. So we were down to two firms, and the negotiations would continue.

Later on, we met with another regional manager, who, unlike some of the others, didn't fit the image at all. He was kind, gracious, and talkative, and we all got along. He took particular interest in me, but in a more genuine way it seemed. He expressed his appreciation for continuity, especially in that business, and he thought that we could form a good long-term partnership, with me eventually taking the helm. So in that respect, my development and input would be paramount to a successful endeavor. I was able to communicate a bit more freely in those meetings, and, although still lacking somewhat, my performances were much better than most of my other ones.

The branch we would be working at was to undergo construction on a new wing, so as a sweetener for the deal, they tossed in two huge, brand-new offices with views of the city skyline. It worked. We would finish up negotiations with the local manager, and the lawyers for both sides would soon finalize the contracts. We would plan diligently for the next few months and would make the transition shortly thereafter.

By that time, I had co-signed the contract for the new-construction unit with my father. However, I would have to wait about a year and a half to take delivery. Although the contract signing process was fairly simple, I pulled the same deal as with the wedding testimonial. I went into an office in the back of the sales center and tried to read every word of the thick document. After about half an hour, and only a few pages in, I finally caved and signed.

Now that I think about it, this ritual was a remnant of some of the whispering directives. I was to read every word of every document placed before me, no matter how long it took. If not, in would come the banging. Many of these reading, writing, thinking, and speaking directives had always been around to some degree or another, but thankfully most of them had desisted considerably by the time I signed the contract for the unit.

In any case, I still had to find a place to live in for the interim, so I returned to the old but still fancy building on the lake, which just happened to be right across the street from the new construction. I found a listing, co-signed the loan, and began the move. My mother would help me buy a huge king-size bed with a plush mattress, and I snagged the fancy clothes dressers from my old room, along with my parents' old living room couch and an antique glass coffee table. After all, I had arrived.

I now lived in a beautiful condo overlooking the city and the lakefront drive, but sadly, I still didn't have many friends at all to invite over to share in the experience. Some family did end up coming over here and there during the summer, though. My first cousin on my father's side and her husband made the road trip to visit us, and I brought them downtown. I hadn't really gotten to know her growing up, and it was a treat to reconnect.

They were natural. They were real people. She was a lawyer and he a businessman, but they had no airs to put on. And I liked that. I liked our conversations. We had much in common, and I was still in the process of learning why. We took in a ballgame and trekked around the city a bit.

I had lived in the suburbs of my home city for most of my life and had been downtown for the preceding few years. But even then I still didn't know a whole lot about what the city had to offer. Although I had been out and about somewhat over the years, it was mostly to bars I couldn't remember where and to random apartments with real estate agents.

I took them to a few touristy places and experienced much of it for the first time myself. I was embarrassed about that, so I just tried to play it off. But they seemed to have a good time, and I was finally beginning to interact again in a meaningful way.

CHAPTER EIGHT

Work, Wine, and Women

BIG THINGS WERE COMING UP, and my father and I still had to prepare for the transition. At the house, we held more secret meetings with staff at the house to get things together. My father also enlisted the help of a cousin on my mother's side to aid with logistics and mailing. And, interestingly enough, my old buddy who I had let the doors of the train close on so many years before came back and helped out as well. He had just finished business school and was happy to help as he tried to get a foothold on a new career.

So we all met up at the house, made our way to the office, and unpacked. Paper was everywhere. We sifted through hundreds of envelopes and thousands of documents. My cousin, my friend, my mother, and I stayed at the office late-night and stuffed. The names of clients started to jumble together, and we'd begin to toss out nicknames for them. We got giddy and laughed uncontrollably at times. I thought of the conveyor-belt scene in an old-time sitcom. Things were getting better.

After plowing through the math and logic qualification exams that the firm required, I signed the documents with management. I was now formally employed and would actually be receiving a salary—a good one at that.

However, the firm had a mandatory training program that I would still have to pass to make it to the ranks of a true professional. But, since my father was a top senior producer, many of the nagging formalities like business plans and team leadership meetings luckily did not apply to me. I had a safe wing to hide behind should the firm try to crack the whip or initiate a "molding" process. I was being groomed to jump over the customary hoops instead of through them.

The move was particularly onerous on my father, who had to contact hundreds of clients for both phone and in-person meetings to fully explain the transition. To help facilitate the process, my brother came back from his city to make some calls to clients, as he had worked with my father for several years after college and knew many of them personally. And the endless stream of paperwork and technical data entry was a handful for the assistants to say the least. One of them was literally pulling her hair out. But almost all of the clients came over to the new firm, probably in record time. The transition had been a success.

But my role in all of it was somewhat less visible, simply because I didn't do much. I spoke to a few people here and there, but I didn't have the experience, the knowhow, or the communicative ability at the time to be a real asset to the team. So I shut the door to my small office in our somewhat dreary temporary digs and focused on the training program.

First on the agenda was passing the licensing exam to sell securities professionally. Intermingled with that was the training program. I had a quota of fifty hours of work a week, including daily tasks to complete along the way. I liked to read the lengthy educational pieces explaining the ins and outs of the securities industry, the financial markets, and the broader economy. Although I was learning much of what I should have learned in my economics major track in college, I was gobbling it up nevertheless.

I didn't take the "best practices" material and assigned homework too seriously, though. It seemed a little boilerplate, and plus much of it wouldn't even apply to me, as I would already be starting pretty much on top. So door closed, day after day, I tried to fulfill my time-sheet requirements by memorizing the licensing material backwards and forwards.

Some unwanted thoughts crept in here and there, and since I was in my own space with the door closed, I let the tears flow on many occasions. I thought I was doing a decent job wiping them away and smiling when anyone knocked and walked in. By that time, I felt that I was pretty experienced at hiding my condition from the world.

A few weeks into the training program, the firm flew our group of incoming advisers out to corporate headquarters in the big city for our first interactive training session. It was my first real business trip, and that meant something.

Many of the others in the group had had some solid experience in sales and were much more knowledgeable about the industry than I was coming in. So I'd have to work hard and just try to keep up. I took it seriously. Unfortunately, though, I still wasn't talking much in social situations. And being foreign to the professional atmosphere tamped down my expression even further.

I would go to classes all day and study at night in the hotel. While many of the others in my group went partying in the big city all night, I was fast asleep by mid-evening. I was able to connect with a few people, but as I wasn't partaking in the social options with others, the awkwardness was still fairly thick. And I was performing somewhat poorly in the interactive sessions as well. So to say the least, although I did realize that I was just getting my feet wet, I still came back home a little shaken.

Pretty strung out, I spent my nights alone in the condo, turning in as early as possible. Even when my favorite sports team made the playoffs, which was a huge deal for them, I turned off the TV to get the rest I needed for the next early morning. When my brother called to ask me if I had seen the game the night before, he must have been shocked to hear that I hadn't. I had followed sports all of my life, and I was a nut for my hometown teams. I knew that these games were enormous for the city, but I had to get serious. It was time to get down to business…

Back at the office, I continued to study the material for the licensing exams. I passed the first one without too much of a problem and moved on to tackle the securities advice license. It was a shorter study period, and I passed with about the same decent safety cushion as the first one. Next on the schedule were the two insurance exams, and those came and went without a hitch as well.

At this point, I had actually become somewhat of a professional, at least on paper. I had the credentials to give legal and securities advice, and I could sell securities and insurance to the general public. All things considered, not bad at all.

The next trip to headquarters to round out the training program ran much more smoothly. I had loosened up a little by then and had been having a few glasses of wine on the weekends to take the edge off the stress.

I remember one day in particular during the training week rather clearly. We were all summoned together and ushered into a large classroom with many levels of seating. All of the spaces had phones on the desk tables. We were to take a list of real phone numbers and simply call random people to try to sell our services. The dreaded "cold-calling" model.

Although I had no real services to sell, I had heard my father give his presentation to clients several times before and had gotten the gist. I brazenly picked up the phone and dialed the first number on the list. I had absolutely no idea what I was doing, but surprisingly, it was kind of fun. And, although some of the folks were somewhat curt with me (as is often commonplace with cold-calling), none of them lashed out angrily at me. Some of them actually bought my jive, and a couple of people even asked for a return call down the road. I didn't bring in any new clients, but the experience certainly kick-started my confidence nevertheless.

For the final project, we were tasked with preparing a mock financial analysis for a client and presenting it on tape. I went into the presentation fairly nervous, mostly because of the camera. But I actually did all right and was praised for my improvement. The final written exam seemed a little difficult, and I hadn't seen some of the material before, but a "pass" without a point total would be more than sufficient.

But almost as importantly, I was finally able to connect with a few of my fellow trainees. This time I partook in the festivities and had a few drinks with the others. I had actually begun to have a little fun for the first time in years, probably going all the way back to first semester of law school. Things had, in fact, gotten better. I had left the office a nervous wreck and returned a producing financial adviser with an actual business card.

Back home, I began to sit in on a few meetings with my father and his clients, but I didn't have much of a chance to talk while my father was on a roll with his presentation. So I just sat there most of the time soaking up information. Plus, my input probably would have been detrimental at the time. I could see that, because when I did speak, people weren't always fully receptive. I was once again being billed as a brilliant lawyer (fully licensed in securities this time), but I don't think the product quite matched up with the paper resumé just yet. But, even though a few of our clients must have been a little unimpressed initially, I knew that I had to start somewhere.

It was also quite a difficult office dynamic with my father's assistants. They had been with him for several years and knew his business well—much better than I did. Although I did have the credentials at that point, I was sure that they could still sense the green in me. And although I was technically their boss, the office wasn't going to run exactly like that.

But I got along well with the youngest of the three assistants, who had only been with my father for about two years at the time. She was respectful to me, and I to her, and she took her professional role very seriously. Although we weren't working together too much, things went smoothly when we did. Fortunately for her, but unfortunately for me, she soon got the opportunity to be a lead assistant with another adviser. And even though she left the team before we moved into our fancy new digs, she would still be someone I could talk to, even if it was hard to chat with many of the others in the office.

It was especially difficult at first because much of the same strange and silent behavior from years past had spilled over into my initial interactions with office staff and personnel. And, just as I had found out rather quickly in some of the client meetings, first impressions are sometimes indelible.

My friend who had helped us with the move decided to stay on with the team, and he took the third desk in our new work area after the other assistant left. He would be the right- hand man to my father for technology, spreadsheets, and presentation materials.

Although I didn't collaborate much with my friend on his projects, I did become more and more present at my father's client meetings as the year drew on. After hearing his pitch over and over to many of the hundreds of clients, I began to see more clearly what the business was about. The presentations would sometimes shift a little, based on changing economic conditions, but the core was largely the same. And I was still learning.

I spent a lot of my time reading the research pieces that our firm and the other outlets published to get a feel for the financial markets and its underpinnings. It would turn out to be my main activity, aside from client meetings, for that first stretch. So as I became more and more familiar with the industry, I eventually began to have some substantive input that I could inject into to the discussions here and there.

And, although I think my father might have been a little hesitant with the tag-team approach based on previous results, I continued to force my way in a little and made some connections. Much of what I was saying made sense, at least to me, and it started to roll off the tongue much more fluidly than ever before.

But the social life was still pretty much nonexistent. Many nights I sat alone in my luxurious apartment just thinking—sometimes about business, but often about my personal situation. The few glasses of wine I was having on the weekends soon turned into a few glasses of wine on the weekdays. It made me feel much better, and my thoughts would become clearer. Not to mention the whispering would die down a lot with the drink. I soon made it a practice of pacing around my apartment and talking to myself out loud. With a few drinks in me, I sounded pretty good, like a real professional and a logical, sane thinker.

One night over the summer, my friend who was working with us invited me to a party at his place, and I met a bunch of his friends. But it wasn't just about meeting people. I was able to communicate with them—on their level, and in their reality. I'd still have my whispering thoughts, symbols, and signals going on in my head from time to time, but I somehow found a way to keep it to a subtext and not to play it as the major storyline.

The party at my friend's apartment turned into another group get-together a few nights later, and this time I was ecstatic to finally invite some people over to my place. One of my buddy's friends brought another friend/co-worker along that night to the condo. She was a traveling consultant from overseas and would only be there for a few weeks. And she was gorgeous. I would turn most of my attention in her direction, and we got to talking and laughing.

But as I was opening another bottle of wine in the kitchen, she asked me a question from the living room. I had heard it but pretended I didn't. She was simply commenting on how nice my glass coffee table was and wanted to know where I had gotten it.

Boy was I embarrassed. All of that stuff had come directly from my parents' house. And I was supposed to be on my own now. I had a job, a salary, and my own place. I had grown up by then and wanted desperately to cut the cord. So I stupidly ignored the second question. And the third. I'm sure she knew very well that I could hear her. Awkward.

The group was getting ready to go home, and I decided to walk out with them. Most of them were going different ways, and the girl I had been talking to was headed back to her hotel by herself. The rain had been persistent throughout the night, and she asked me how she could find a cab. I offered to find her one and drop her off. She smiled and agreed.

Soaking wet, we hopped into the cab for the short ride to her hotel. Once there, I felt that I should say something. Something charming.

"Just ask for her number. Anything. Quick."

But she said her goodbye, her gracious thank you, and closed the door behind her.

Failure sank in. I would see her at another party soon after, but with minimal conversation. I felt uncomfortable, and it probably shone clear. I wouldn't see her again after that.

I knew I had to continue to turn things around. So I started to learn some of the ins and outs of wine, cheeses, paté, and French bread. I had to make a good impression on everyone who walked through the door. I had to look like I knew what I was doing, even if I really had no clue.

One day I bumped into a girl I had gone to grade school and junior high with, and we had a nice chat. She seemed interested and gave me her phone number. I thought about it a lot and finally gave it a shot. We had coffee and talked, and she came by to see the place. I drank some wine, but she decided not to. And although the chatting became a little easier for me, I could tell that she was holding back a little.

I would see her only few more times, in large part because my mind was still a little lost. I talked to her occasionally on the phone, and she would tell me many months down the road that she really regretted not having that glass of wine with me. She had always been pleasant and nice to be with, but even then I knew it wasn't going to work. So, although I was still starved for interaction, I decided not to press the issue.

The wine began to flow more and more as the summer drew on. The few glasses on the weekdays turned into about a bottle. I settled in at a bottle and an extra glass as my limit. I could still get up without a huge hangover and make it to work on time and functional. And I figured that the wine was nowhere near as bad as the hard liquor that I used to guzzle down years before.

One particular night after a few drinks, I was feeling lonely as hell. So I called my father's sister who I hadn't really spoken to much in ages. We had a fantastic conversation and caught up on life. The words were fluid, and we began to talk often from then on.

A huge election was coming up, and over the previous year or so, I had developed a keen interest in politics. I had been somewhat informed since law school, but I began to take it to the next level. Ideas began to form freely about the condition of the country and our society. Those thoughts spilled over into notions of global cohesiveness and maintaining justice for all human beings. I was developing an individual perspective, a worldview of sorts.

So my aunt and I continued to chat many times well into the night about policy, the future of our nation, and the sound bites and gaffes of the politicians jockeying for position. I was finally able to express an intellectual opinion about something I had actually thought about. And I had constructed it on my own. I felt I did it well, and I was getting better with every chat.

Around the same time, I started to find interest in certain types of clothes, particular art, and various other items that people generally make purchasing decisions about. And I began to notice subtle differences in the wine I was drinking. I couldn't drink the cheap stuff anymore. I needed a good label. I also found that I liked good cheese—and not the sliced and processed kind. My new taste required the esoteric names from overseas.

Finally, the construction of my unit had been completed, and I was ready to move in. Back when we signed the contract, I had the great fortune of picking out all the rough and finish selections for the condo. Of course, I had to have the granite and wood. But I went even a step further than that with the marble and the steam shower in the bathroom. And the view. Astounding. Balcony shots of fireworks on the lake were going to be awesome. It was incredible that we went in blind and got such a good deal. However we did it, it definitely worked out.

The wine continued to flow at the new apartment. But the stir craziness of drinking alone all the time finally got to me. One night, after a good amount of wine, I ventured out onto the street to see if I could find a place to drink and meet people. Anywhere would do, I just had to get out of the house.

So I wandered around for a bit and eventually found my way to a local neighborhood bar with some sports flags waving outside. Once inside, the stairs brought me down to a lower-level floor. It was a large place with a huge oval bar, plenty of eating space, and yes, three glorious pool tables.

I continued to frequent that particular bar fairly frequently over the next few weeks, and I got to know a few of the bartenders and some of the staff. One day as I was racking up the billiard balls, I noticed two girls standing nearby. Having had a few, I had no qualms about asking them if they wanted to play a friendly game of pool. They were hesitant, so I decided to improvise.

One of the girls had a clear accent from somewhere overseas. I had heard a similar sound from some family members in the past, but this one was a little different. I couldn't quite place it. I asked them if they would play a game with me if I were able to guess her country of origin. They laughed, agreed, and wished me luck. I tossed out the name of an obscure nation close to my relatives' home country on my mother's side—a pretty aimless shot in the dark. They froze in total bewilderment. Out came the sticks and the chalk.

We played for while, and I struck up a conversation with the other girl. She was pretty, and I was totally winging it. Somehow things started to flow like that. No real mistakes, no discomfort, almost no awkwardness whatsoever. Before they left, she gave me her number and told me to call her. I would certainly do so.

We had a few nice dinners at some spots in the city I had been wanting to go to. As I already knew very well, it's hard to do anything but takeout by yourself. And in any case, tables for one were getting old. So I enjoyed walking in with someone and having the hostess seat us in a proper way. I won't lie, though, it did feel a little weird. I don't know if I'd ever even been on a real date in my adult life prior to that one. It was a good thing, but still a little strange at first.

So we went out three or four times, and after the last date, I invited her back to my place. I had just been shopping that day, and I hadn't put away all of the items. Big mistake. I had gotten an economy-size package of Kleenex boxes for some reason that day. I always over-shopped. She asked why I needed all of that Kleenex, and I didn't have a good answer. Uncomfortable silence. She left soon after.

But knowing that the stupid Kleenex probably wasn't a deal-breaker, the next day I tried to go the extra mile. I found a nice array of flowers online and ordered it. The pop-up window prompted me for size, and I impetuously picked large. Now that *was* a mistake. Not to mention the fact that I sent them to her office at the hotel where she was working. She had a managerial position there, and I'm sure she was fully embarrassed.

Looking back, it was a little early and over the top for sure. I spoke to her later, and she thanked me, but I think she was still pretty wary about the flowers. She also told me that she was heading back to the suburbs to be with her parents for a while. She stopped returning my calls.

That fall, my favorite team was the best in baseball, and I was damn sure not about to miss the playoffs this time. Although I watched them at home alone, I saw every minute.

But sports weren't the only thing occupying my mind. The election was in a few weeks, and I was all in. I watched all of the news stories and hung on to every word of the debates. I deconstructed their policy positions and often shouted at the TV. And, although I talked about the issues a lot with my aunt and my other family members, I kept it quiet at work for the most part. I was getting better at client communication, but that certainly wasn't the time or place for politics.

But I continued to find substance in things. I had begun to have many of the same thoughts about life during law school, but I just wasn't able to verbalize them. Just like with foreign language in college, it took me a few years out of law school to really grasp a lot of what I learned. I had managed to find some sense of perspective by then, and things made more sense set against a larger backdrop. I was outside the vacuum, and I was rolling.

Notions of justice, peace, righteousness, and prudent thought and behavior dominated my consciousness. How to better society through sound planning and decisive action was a common topic of conversation, both internally and with others. I was finding out more about what I knew even before I knew it.

"This is what *I* think," I was finally able to say.

I had never seen the world like that before.

So I now had a vision. But I was still deeply, deeply alone. I hadn't had a real girlfriend since high school. And she was the only one that I had ever had. I tried the speed-dating thing a few times and met some interesting people, but no luck. I had run out of options, and it was time to shake things up a little bit.

So I went on the internet and found a professional dating service. I was making enough money to afford it. In fact, the one thing I couldn't afford anymore was the loneliness. So I met with the coordinator, and she gave me the standard pitch, with a discount option for immediate payment by cash or check. Hook, line, and sinker.

Buyer's remorse eventually set in that week.

"This is a helluva lot of money," I figured, "and I could probably find someone on my own, right?"

I wrote the cancellation letter on time, but because of the weekend, they purportedly didn't receive it until after the deadline. They declined my request, and I felt cheated. I came to the conclusion that it was probably some kind of a racket. I got flustered and called to complain. I talked to the coordinator, and things got a little heated.

It was one of the only times I could remember in my new life that I got so upset as to become confrontational. The lawyer in me peeked out and tossed small claims court onto the table. But I quickly reeled it in and settled the horses. This was not the way to go about anything. It wasn't me.

So I called back the next day and apologized for getting a little frustrated, and we agreed to continue the service. They would set me up with several girls over the next year or so, and I was finally "dating" again, even though it didn't feel like the real thing. And I knew it wasn't. But I still tried and ended up meeting some nice girls. It seemed pretty clear to me that most of them were pretty much in the same lonely boat as I was, but we did have some pleasant dinners, and I threw on whatever charm I had to offer.

Surprisingly, the first few girls were pretty receptive. They gave me great reviews with the coordinator and wanted to continue dating. But it just wasn't there for me. I could have dragged it along for the hell of it, but I didn't want to be a user. That wasn't me either. Soon after the first few dates, though, I had to put the setups on hold for a little while. Something had come up.

CHAPTER NINE

Understanding

MY BROTHER HAD FOUND a new position in the city he lived in and would have a few weeks off before he would start the new gig. So he called me and asked if I was up for an excursion. He thought it would be a perfect time to travel a bit and see the world. I was game.

I had lost contact with my brother for several years after he left for boarding school way back when. I was still in junior high school, and we had had some vicious fights growing up. The sour feelings spilled over into young adulthood, and when he went away, we had little to do with each other's lives. We rarely talked, and when we went on family vacations, there was a wall between us most of the time. We would acknowledge each other and have a few decent interactions, but there was no real connection there. This continued all throughout college and for several years thereafter.

It wasn't until he became engaged and got married that we attempted to reconnect. But the truth is that I hadn't really been talking to anyone for a long time before that, so those years when I was in law school were lost on us anyway. In any case, it took a while, but we slowly got reacquainted. And this trip would be a good way to speed up the process. So we planned to fly to the other side of the globe to visit a country rich in culture and history that neither of us had been to before.

My brother arranged for travel guides and tours, and he sent me the proposed itinerary of events. I read the schedule and immediately knew that it was not about to work. Four-hour flights followed by five-hour drives all over the country, basically for two weeks straight. It would have been fantastic to see the whole country and experience everything it had to offer, but I knew what my sleep meant to me. And I think the doctors were right on this one as well. Only a few hours of shut eye here and there for two weeks could be a dangerous proposition.

So, jokingly, I told my brother that he was going to "murder" me with the schedule. He laughed, understood my concerns, and said that we could change the itinerary as we saw fit. So we boarded the plane, looking forward to business class for fifteen hours—fully reclining seats, champagne, and all the movies you could ever want, including the new releases. I still don't really know exactly how we got those seats, but my brother did mention something about finagling our spots by taking advantage of a gimmick challenge that the airline was offering at the time. Anyway, he managed to get it done, and we were on our way.

The guide met us promptly at the airport, and we headed to the hotel. People were everywhere. Speeding cars whipped around the streets inches apart from each other. Oh, and elephants and cows were right in the middle of some of the lanes, too. And the honking. The incessant honking. Many of the cars had no side mirrors so as to be able to get by the other ones on the road without hitting them. So they'd just honk at each other to signal their presence. The buses even had signs on the rear: *Honk, please.* What an unmitigated mess. Happily, though, the whispering thoughts weren't too ramped up at the time. But the honking didn't make matters any better. I fought through the headache.

We toured around for a few days, listened intently to some interesting history lessons, and trekked around some ancient landmarks. I could see all of it, and I found it intellectually stimulating, mostly the human history. But I couldn't *feel* it. I used to remember what the sights and sounds would do. And the smells. Especially the smells. I can still faintly remember those distinct smells I picked up in the foreign countries I visited in college. They have an effect on you. They help you to feel. They help you to be. It's part of the human experience. But at that time I couldn't sense any of that. I still enjoyed watching from afar, nevertheless, and we would be traveling again soon.

We ordered the best car the company could offer—a veritable beater with halfway-running air condition. We were off. We soon found the highway where we would be able to pick up some time. It was a bumpy dirt road, featuring some pedestrians and cows that would intermittently pass through the middle of speeding traffic.

"Just grip the side of the car and hang on," I told myself.

As our driver weaved around the moving obstacles, I began to get a bearing of my surroundings. My grip tightened, and my knuckles whitened. Poverty. Abject, unadulterated poverty. Dilapidated shanty huts of tin and wood graced the sides of the dusty road. Meager possessions—buckets, pots, and tires—littered the shoulders. Filth everywhere. Sad eyes and sagging skin. Daily chores of survival. I had never seen anything like this before in my life.

"Just get there. Don't even think about the car hitting a bump and losing a tire."

I tried to squeeze the thought right out of my head, but more thoughts just popped in.

"Would they be violent? Would they steal everything we had? Were we in danger? Would we ever get back home? Four hours of this?!"

We finally found our way onto some side streets, which, by the way, weren't much better than the highway. But soon I could tell that we were almost there. As we approached the large metal gates, we were greeted by a couple of sharply dressed uniformed guards. After a quick search, we rolled in. This was a real, paved driveway. Grass was actually growing on the sides of the street. Right in the middle of all of that filth—a painstakingly manicured palace resort. And even though this place certainly didn't look like it fit in the middle of all that, I didn't want to ask for any explanations. I was spent, and more than that, incredibly thankful to have gotten there safely. The welcoming party offered us an exotic juice drink and graced us with their culture's traditional greeting. But we would have to get a good night's sleep. We would be seeing one of the wonders of the world the next day.

It was a glorious, shining, white structure, and it amazed me that it had been built so long ago. I marveled at the time and energy that must have been involved in such a production. Our guide snapped a photo of us in the middle of the meticulously aligned pathway that led directly up to the symmetrical structure. My father would later blow this picture up to epic proportions, frame it, and hang it proudly in his vacation home living room.

The road back to the city was anything but the same. The sights had changed. Over the span of two days, the country had completely transformed before my eyes. As we made our way back onto the highway, I noticed a group of schoolchildren on the side of the road skipping off to morning classes. Something struck me. Their uniforms were immaculate. Bright white pristine shirts, ironed skirts and slacks, and colorful backpacks neatly fastened in place.

"Where in the world are they coming from?" I wondered.

The sun shone down on us as we zipped along the mostly empty road. A sense of calm passed over me. This ride wouldn't be so bad after all.

That same day we flew to a city on the coast. When we got into the cab, I couldn't believe my ears. No honking. No dirt. Clean streets with modern-looking cars. Actual shops on the side of the road. Shopkeepers sweeping the sidewalks. Cement and paved roads.

"I could live with this," I thought.

After exploring some ancient ruins off the coast, we stopped in an exclusive hotel for lunch. An array of exquisitely prepared foods from all over the world lay in front of us, buffet style. And it was "all-you-can-eat." Long gone were the days of frozen lean dinners in front of the television. I would partake.

Next we flew to a resort area up the coast for some relaxation. We had a quaint little bungalow and enjoyed some peace and quiet. I hadn't had much to drink on the trip, so I decided to order a bottle of wine to help make the atmosphere a little more enjoyable. One glass turned into a few, and I got to thinking. My brother came home from a run, and I tried to strike up a conversation. I made a comment about the expansiveness of the universe and the billions upon billions of stars that are projected to be out there.

"There must be a 'Goldilocks' planet like ours out there. And if there are many, there must be a good chance that intelligent life exists elsewhere."

He got up without saying anything, took the bottle, went to the sink, and poured it down the drain. I knew that these thoughts were not illogical. I had had many of these types of discussions with my aunt and uncle over the preceding year or so, and they surely got it. I had been able to refine my thought process, and I had a foothold on reality, even if one leg was still in the netherworld. And I didn't appreciate the approach either. But I did see the point. And it would become clearer to me over time.

When we got back to the city where we had initially arrived, a gentleman from the travel agency was waiting for us in the lobby. To our surprise, he pulled a huge wad of cash out of his pocket and handed it to my brother. We hadn't taken many of the flights or car rides we had reserved and hadn't stayed at some of the hotels on our itinerary. We hadn't even discussed cancellation policies, and frankly, we weren't sure if the company had had any to begin with. But the man showed us the itemized bill and explained the reimbursement. I began to see much more clearly now that not all people and cultures fit neatly into the confining boxes that we often create for them…

Back at the office, I was having trouble settling in. My parents were beginning to spend more and more time at the vacation condo they had bought, which was across the country on the shore. It was a fantastic environment—sun, beach, pool, golf, and great restaurants. It was a slower pace out there, but my father was still able to get his work done. He had access to the firm's remote system, could pull up client accounts, and would always be able to take phone appointments.

But I was still at the office in the suburbs, and it was getting harder and harder every day to find things to do to keep busy. This was especially the case at the time, because we hadn't been having as many in-person meetings as regularly as before. And there was only so much industry research out there to read. To add to the complications, another one of our assistants who I had gotten along with pretty well had left a few months before to work with another adviser at a different firm. Although we quickly found a replacement, the working relationship with this new assistant wouldn't be as smooth.

As it were, the senior assistant who was still with us didn't seem to take to me very well either. She was still pulling her hair out, while "daddy's boy" could come and go as he pleased. And it seemed to put a strain on my relationship with my friend from school as well. He was still working with us, and although he did have his regular tasks, he was also doing a lot of secretarial work for the team. This seemed a little out of place to me, as he had shown me some of the more complex work he had done in business school a while before. But, although I could tell that something didn't fit there, he seemed to be working pretty hard and getting along well anyway.

He was also still sitting in one of the cubicles outside our offices, so I'm sure he got a hefty dose of the office gossip. I'm not exactly sure what he was thinking about me, but he was good at bonding with the other assistants, and from what I could tell, he seemed to share in their general perspective. Also, it didn't help matters that for the first year or so, my cognition capabilities were still slowly on the way back. It was sometimes harder for me than others to understand the firm's systems and to get a grasp on the right technique. Admittedly, I wasn't very productive at first, and my guess is that those first impressions of competence probably resonated with my friend and the other assistants alike.

In any case, the new assistant was a go-getter. She knew the systems and the process, having worked with the firm for quite a while. And my father trusted her implicitly. So, although I was well on my way back to reality, I still didn't have the technical skills or the same familiarity with the firm that she did. But, thankfully, I was able to do my own independent work. I dealt with client communication, did research for our presentations to clients, and was given an account to get my feet wet managing money.

Still, though, our assistants' and my decision-making paths would often cross. Daily issues would have to be dealt with, and someone would have to make executive decisions when my father wasn't in the office. And I often embraced a different approach to the business than my assistants did. So my father would have to make some painstaking choices. Unfortunately, though, most of the time the competence contest was not so favorable to me. I dealt with some frustrating condescension from the assistants, often veiled in passive-aggressive comments. And many times the comments weren't veiled at all. But I chose not to lose my cool, and I would hold firm on that decision. I would treat them all with courtesy, offer a jovial "Good morning" every time I walked in, and I would just deal. I vowed to be kind and respectful, even if I wasn't getting the same treatment in return. I would feel the brunt of the losing end of many power plays, but I wouldn't lash out. Rather, I would try to *understand* it.

"What's really going on here?" I would ask myself. "Why do people act this way? I don't think I deserve poor treatment, but, again, what's the *cause*?"

Once I delved deeper into cause and effect, I began to realize something. Most people don't just wake up one day and decide they're going to be mean and nasty to people. No, many times they don't even realize what they're doing. Much of this is learned behavior. Many of these people have themselves been harmed in one way or another and are simply passing that feeling along to others—not because they decide to rationally, but because it makes them feel better. Dishing it out sometimes helps them to function.

In essence, we are all simply products of our environment to some degree or another. If we condemn each other simply because of our shortcomings and idiosyncrasies and don't look to the root of our problems, then we are completely missing the point. If we impetuously write each other off, then our myopia has gotten the better of us.

But more importantly, we must look inside to see the truth. What are we actually doing, how are we doing it, and why? It's easy to make snap judgments. But in the end, we are only condemning ourselves. We've all been there. We've all felt it. The human condition is too common to all of us. And if we know how it feels, if we know why it happens, and most importantly, if we know it's what we've also done, then what right do we have to condemn at all? We often lose sight. We often detach. We look outside without first turning in. It's easier on our ego that way.

Now all of that is easy to say, but how easy is it to convert those ideas into productive behavior? Not very. Every time I was dismissed or passed over by someone, I could feel it in my gut.

But I had to slow down and ask myself, "Do I really have the right answer, or am I just trying to play the part?"

Every time we sat in a client meeting and I was cut off or someone talked over me, it definitely hit me. But was what I wanted to say really a good thing for the business? It wouldn't have been right to risk losing our clients' trust, which my father had garnered for over a quarter-century, simply because his young son wanted to play too.

But things weren't that simple either. I was learning. And I was getting better. I was figuring out how to act and how to interact again. I did have some good ideas, and I was becoming more and more intimately familiar with the markets and the economy every day. We had just gone through one of the worst disasters the financial markets had ever seen. We were on the precipice of depression. People had lost a lot of wealth. I mean a *lot*. This wasn't a joke. These were serious times, and there were serious repercussions for our actions. We were professionals, and our clients needed us. And my father knew his business and the industry—backwards and forwards. He knew his clients and what they wanted and needed. And he knew how to provide service to them. So reasonably, he held firmly onto the helm.

To add to the tension, our visions of how the business would transition to me over time were vastly different. And this became much more apparent to me as time went on. As I saw it, I was being highlighted as one of two intelligent and capable partners. My idea of a productive operation involved open communication, close collaboration, and joint presentation. As I got to know the clients, we would be a team.

But my father had done it his way all his life, and there was no mistaking that he was very successful at it. After all, his livelihood, my career, and our clients' futures were all at stake, and the risk was too great. So, eventually, I came understand that my father saw the transfer of the business as just a baton handoff to me at his retirement.

I began to have doubts.

"Is this what I really want to do with my life? Is this the right occupation for me? Is this something I can do over the long term?"

The industry we were in involved so much falsity, so much dishonesty and corruption, so much taking advantage of people. The whole world had witnessed it firsthand over the previous two years or so.

But then again, my father's business was legitimate. He provided a good service to good people. They couldn't do it without him, and I would hear that from them over and over again in our meetings. Some wouldn't just praise him; they would thank God that he was taking care of them. It really was that intense. He had done well by people in a decent way. I could see that he was somewhat of an anomaly in that industry. Knowing all of that still didn't make me much happier at work, but understanding the situation did ease my stress a bit, and it would get me through stretches here and there. Over time, though, the doubts would slowly keep eating away at me.

The last thing I wanted to do was burst my father's bubble. He had put so much time and effort into building that business, and I knew that he always wanted to pass it along to one of his sons. Not to mention that I was looking dead straight into a crazy amount of money in the future. I figured that I would basically have independent financial security for the rest of my life in ten years or so. I knew that I would have to make a decision soon.

So I did some serious thinking.

"What do I like to do? What am I good at? But more importantly, what drives me? What's my passion?"

I was having difficulties there. I thought to myself some more.

"Well, I'm pretty good at research. I like poring over documents, analyzing them, and constructing worthwhile and substantive pieces of work. I can write. I can understand a logical progression and make a pretty sound argument. I can write."

“What kind of a job description encapsulates all of that? No listings on career sites on the internet even come close. And even so, most of the good jobs require a decent amount of work experience just to get a foot in the door. I certainly don’t want to get boxed in at some dead-end job for the rest of my life. I know my opinions matter, but what can I write about? I think I still need some more experience. Actually, I wouldn’t mind going back to school again.”

So I kind of fell backwards into the decision: I’d apply to journalism school.

Soon after, I signed up to take the graduate school qualification exam and picked up an application for one of the most prestigious universities in the country, which happened to be just outside of my city. I’d only apply to one, because I wouldn’t settle for less. I told my father of my decision almost exactly at the same time as his senior assistant gave him notice that she was accepting another position within the office.

Straight into damage control. As if things with the markets weren’t stressful enough for him. The decision was hard for me to swallow as well, but I was still committed to it. I would help him search for a new assistant until admissions decisions came out and would hopefully bow out gracefully. He was nothing but supportive and fully respected my choice. I was surprised that he didn’t try to convince me not to go, but looking back, I probably shouldn’t have been. He shouldn’t have had to tell me that my happiness was at the top of the list of his many concerns.

We would have trouble hiring another assistant for the next several months due to the firm’s cost-cutting measures, so we would have to make do. However, my focus would soon turn elsewhere, and I began to hone in on the exam. After a poor performance on the verbal section of the exam, I knew I would be taking it again. But the second time was the charm this time. My scores were way above average—one of the top percentiles. Once again, though, all I could do was hope that the admissions committee would overlook the poor scores and concentrate on the better ones.

I enlisted the help of a consultant so as to leave nothing to chance. Her time was expensive, but I thought my essays could use a boost. I was utterly shocked at her response to my first drafts. Some serious condescension even filtered in. But only looking back now do I know why. I had by that time lost the concept of writing a good admissions essay. I had been writing in a completely different format and tone for the previous several years, and the essays for this application needed to be anything but formal and verbose. Instead, they required finesse and touch. They had to be both informative and creative. You had to toot your own horn, but not too loud. I still didn't get it. Plus, one of the essays required some extensive knowledge of the journalism industry, of which I had none. Recommendations weren't easy to come by either. I hadn't had many close relationships with my professors, and frankly, my overall grades really weren't that good. But I finally submitted the documents and hoped for the best.

CHAPTER TEN

Unchaining the Social Animal

MEANWHILE, I had been going on the fix-up dates every month or so. I was getting much better, and almost all of the women seemed pretty interested. I was finding out more and more about the city and its popular spots on every date, and I was excited to keep going out. I had begun to break out of the familiar routine of frequenting touristy, somewhat cheesy places mostly reserved for people from out of town. I didn't sense any major connections with any of the women, though. But when one of them asked me on a second date, I accepted—partly because she seemed nice and I didn't want to reject her, and partly because I needed to get out more.

So I found a nice classy spot for a few drinks. It was a hotel bar, but a fancy one with a fireplace and fruity signature cocktails. As we sat down on the cozy plush couch, I could sense her glossy gaze in my direction, and I knew she was feeling frisky. We took a cab back to my place, and she coyly accepted my offer to come upstairs for a nightcap. It was the first time I had had any kind of intimacy with a girl in over five years.

But it still didn't feel right. Afterwards, we fell asleep. I woke up with a girl in my bed after a date for the first time in my life. But all I could think about was how to part ways with her with the least amount of awkwardness possible. It didn't seem like she was too uncomfortable with the whole thing, and she left soon after.

By that time, I had gotten the itch for going out and meeting people. The drink was working, and I was finally beginning to be social again. I would continue to see the doctor who prescribed my medicine every month, as I had done ever since my incident in college. I had become much more talkative, and one day I finally told him about the sexual side effects I had been experiencing after switching over to the oval yellow pill. We went down a little on the dosage, and after no results, he would soon be OK with changing things up a little bit. He scrapped the yellow pill and introduced me to a small light-pink one. This pill would ameliorate the issues I was having with the other medication, and it would soon set me on a course back to more capable cognitive thought.

Within a few weeks of taking the new pill, I felt a little more in tune with things. One night I was staying over at my parents' place alone, as they were at their vacation condo on the coast. Although the condo would soon become their permanent home for most of the year, they were still traveling back and forth a bit. But on this particular night, I was all by myself at the house. And I had a hot tub out back just begging for some action. So I decided to venture out.

By then things had changed a bit. I had ditched the conservative side part, slacks, and button-downs that I had gotten so used to over the years. I had been wearing suits to work every day and had already been going out on semi formal dates with women through the service. So it felt right strutting into the suburban dive bar, hair slicked back and fully suited up—sans tie of course.

I was on a mission. I bought a few drinks for some of the folks at the bar and wedged myself cleanly into a few conversations. I would learn quickly that conversation of any type, no matter what the content was, almost always took the edge off of a solo production. If people didn't see you wandering around by yourself, then you weren't alone. And that's all that mattered.

I looked over and noticed two girls waiting for a drink at the end of the bar—one platinum blonde and one ethnic brunette. I offered to buy them a drink, and we chatted for a while. But as it was getting late, I had to cut to the chase. I told them about the hot tub and gave them a pretty convincing party pitch. They went to the bathroom to talk it over and came back with an affirmative. Pretty soon we were all naked, sipping wine and feeling the bubbles below.

After a while, we got out and dried off. I was inside the house with the brunette, while the blonde went to the bathroom. She opened up the bathrobe I gave her to expose her naked body. I did the same. We laughed. The blonde came back, and now the brunette went to the bathroom. I couldn't wait anymore, so I brought the blonde to a bedroom in the back of the house. It was the same risky behavior as that snowy night so many years before. Then came a loud knock at the door. The brunette was waiting outside and probably feeling left out. I don't know for the life of me why I didn't get up to let her in. I was probably thinking that it might never happen again and that getting up might ruin the moment.

The knocking soon stopped, and we continued. But soon after, the brunette came back and pounded louder. I finally got up and opened the door this time. She must have been out there for a while and was clearly upset. She told me that they had to be at work soon and that they couldn't call in sick that day. And it was already morning. They scooped up their clothes and rushed out the door, one giddy blonde and one pissed-off brunette. The next day I woke up and couldn't find my watch. I thought I had left it outside by the hot tub, but I wasn't sure. The snow would soon cover the area, and the search would be over. I never did find that watch.

Two days later, I got some sad news. The doctor who had been taking care of my medication had passed away suddenly. Although I had been seeing him for over a decade by that time, I had only just begun to converse effectively with him. I walked into the hospital for the funeral and couldn't even get through the front door. The large, lecture hall-type room was packed to the rafters, a long line spilling out into the hallway. I finally got a seat along the wall, but I couldn't see any of the speakers. I would just have to listen. Doctors, patients, professionals, and family—pretty much every speaker—brought tears to the eyes of the mourners. But for me, it was the patients who had the most compelling stories. This doctor had saved lives, and I now knew that.

Things were beginning to get more exciting. The mundane trips to and from work listening to the wonderfully informative but often monotonous public radio transformed into dance party in the car with the latest pop music. Once I got home, I would have a few glasses of wine, don my suit, slick the hair back, and venture out to the neighborhood bar to seek any thrill I could find. I would play pool, mingle with a few folks, and see where the night would take me.

One night I came upon an excitable dude, we shot a little pool, and neither of us was ready to call it quits. He mentioned a late-night place. I was game. I hadn't been to a strip club in a while, but I was basically on autopilot at that point. I was just going with the flow and soaking it all in. We would meet up a few times and roll around town, many times to the bar or to the raunchy clubs. When I asked him his full name so I could put it in my phone contacts, he told me to just enter the word "*Trouble.*" Yup, that's about right.

One night he came by the place, and I popped a bottle of smooth red wine. This was no "Two-Buck Chuck," by the way.

This was the fancy stuff. He suddenly jumped up and said that he would show me a fantastic concoction he loved to drink. I was to trust him that it was nothing but excellent. He poured a large glass of wine and dumped soda in it up to the brim. It tasted like shit. He would soon get engaged, and I wouldn't see him after that. I think he told me that he was writing poetry or something.

I began to head down to the neighborhood bar more and more often, and, although the bar closed pretty late at night, the late-late-night spots were always on my mind. I found a particular one not too far away—another bar with a couple of pool tables. This was a shabbier joint than the regular neighborhood one, but I still liked it, especially for its late hours. One night, I ran into a stout African American dude on the pool table. After a few games, we ended up at another strip club across town. My treat. This would end up happening a lot, and it was always my treat.

The strip joints got me to thinking. After all the bars and the commiserating, I would invariably come home alone, drunk, wired, and frisky. The new pills had rid me of those side effects, and my libido had come back in full force. It was time to finally explore the fantasies I had been dreaming about since adolescence. A few keystrokes and phone calls later, ladies began showing up at my door—all different kinds of people, at all times of the night. At first it was just once in a while, a pretty innocuous "massage." But it soon turned into a regular habit, sometimes several nights a week. Sometimes they were familiar girls, and sometimes new ones with enticing pictures.

It was a routine. I'd have a few glasses of wine, get all jacked up, and head down to the bar. By then I had gotten to know all of the guys there. The door staff always greeted me with a fist bump and a "What's up," and the bartenders would often toss me a shout out as I strolled in. They always had my drink, and no more waiting in line at the bar. It was a home away from home, a place to get away. I was part of a crowd again, and I stood out. It was probably the most fun I had had since early on in college.

One night I was feeling it, so I made my way down the street to the bar. I hopped down the stairs brimming with particular swagger and confidence. I grabbed a stick and looked for takers. No one left, no one right. So as I had started to do on a regular basis, I struck up a random conversation with someone at the bar. I was losing the fear, and the drink would sweep it away even further. This was no ordinary random dude, though. He was African American, bald, and huge. Built like a truck, he towered over me from his barstool.

I tossed out a number. He would understand. It was the amount I was offering to play him for on the pool table. In fact, this was the very first thing I said to him. He let out a deep chuckle. He was in. And I was in, for a drubbing that is. I was a good pool player, actually really pretty good. A couple of drinks would get the ball rolling better, but there was definitely a limit. Any past the threshold, and I was just cracking the balls around, hoping some would go in. I hit the ball too hard. I always hit the ball too damn hard.

But this guy had the touch. He summarily dispensed with me, and my ego.

"Next."

He was probably the best player I had ever seen, aside from my father's brother maybe. But this didn't put a cramp in my style. We chopped it up for a while, and he would be the first dude I'd look for when I'd walk into the bar from then on.

But all of this cost money. The bar tabs, the random strip clubs, the twenties tossed out to all of the staff, the huge tips, the girls coming to the place, and so on and so on. My salary was good, but not that good. I remembered that I had asked my father to borrow a little money a while before. He asked me to take it out of the joint account that he had set up under my mother's and my name. I wasn't exactly sure why it was there or what it was for, but there was a lot of money there. And it had my name on it. Literally. So I took out the first batch without thinking much of it. And I'm not really sure what I was thinking the next time. I had to pay for things, it was there, and like I said, it had my name on it. It went on and on like that. A little here and there turned into a regular monthly deal. It became routine, a sort of self-imposed, unearned supplement to my salary.

Soon afterwards, admissions decisions from the journalism school came in. I had been waitlisted. Not for long, though. And after the final rejection letter came, I would once again have to reevaluate. Many of the same thoughts about my career choice came to mind again, but this time the counterarguments were stronger. I had basically nowhere to go, the job market was in the can, and I had to cover my mortgage and my new expensive habits. Plus, I was able to stroll in and out of the office freely and had a hefty dose of half-days.

But past that, there were some more substantive concerns. My father had pretty much moved to the coast by then, and I had become the point person for much of the activity at the office. We were finally able to hire a new sales assistant to replace the old one, and I was intimately involved in the hiring process. I conducted one-on-one interviews with her, and I had been in on the final decision to hire her. She was genuine, kind, and respectful, and we maintained a good professional working relationship. Whether I liked it or not, I had some sense of responsibility at the office. Although I wasn't necessarily indispensable to the operation, I had gotten to know many of the clients and was beginning to take care of some of them on my own.

And I was helping my father. His stress levels had been through the roof, both with the transition a few years earlier and with the turmoil and shake-up with the staff over time. I knew that I could provide a buffer zone for him with many of the daily activities that wouldn't necessarily need his attention. If I could take care of it, it would lessen his burden, and therefore his stress levels, quite a bit.

“Plus,” I thought, “I might even be able to stick it out for a while—maybe just until my father retires, whenever that would be, or maybe even longer. It might not be a lifetime gig, but I might be able to manage for the time being.”

So I redirected my focus. I would try to gain more credibility and legitimacy within the industry. I certainly didn’t want to be just a hack salesman. I wanted the intellectual approach to investing and money management. None of this “pull-the-wool-over-the-client’s-head-and-squeeze-a-fee-out-of-them” crap. I wanted to do it the right way, the honest way, with integrity, quality, and substance. If I were to do this, I wanted to be serious about it. So I began the study courses for the most relevant and advanced professional designation that I could find. And I went to work on it. It would occupy my time, and I felt like I was being productive. I was still letting loose in the city quite a bit, but I came into the office and got my studying done. I was determined to make it work.

Although my friend was still working with our team, our relationship had undergone considerable strain over the preceding few years. I think he had been grappling with many of the same issues as I was struggling with about the industry. Plus, his working relationship with my father wasn’t the best either. He eventually decided to follow the track for becoming an adviser, and it was a tough dynamic for all of us. But one night he did contact me and asked if I wanted to go out with him and a few of his friends from business school. I hadn’t been out with him in a long time, and it was good to actually be with a group and walk into a bar with other people for once.

We made our way into a crowded clubby joint and mingled around. The place was abuzz, and the music was thumping. It was a social scene for social people. As I slid my way through a group of dancing girls en route to our spot in the back, I recognized someone. She was an old friend from way back in the day. I had known her and her brother from my hometown, our families knew each other, and we used to meet up at the tennis club over the summers with my cousin. And actually, she had been close with my brother after they graduated college. They were both living in the city at the time and used to hang out within the same circle of friends.

So it was surprising to just run into her at a bar in the big city like that. We hugged and chatted for a while. Turned out she had become a social mastermind of sorts. She was great at bringing people together for parties and events and generally connecting with people. She knew exactly how to forge and maintain lasting relationships with people from all different walks of life.

So we got reacquainted, and she told me that she was running a networking-type organization that hosted get-togethers for professionals from my father's particular ethnic background every month. She suggested that I come along to their next soiree.

"Why not?" I thought.

It would be fantastic, not only to get to know people in the city, but to try to reconnect with some of my roots which I had neglected basically my whole life. I really had no identification or sense of connection with the two different cultures my parents had come from. I hadn't done any investigation. I hadn't made the effort. So I went.

I walked in not knowing anyone except for my friend, who was the host. But the introductions were quick, and I made new connections pretty easily. I met two doctors who not only seemed intelligent, but who also looked like they knew very well how to have a good time. We would all end up going out late-night that night. The drinks kept coming, and things were good. The doctors and I would continue to go out with the rest of the group late into the night, many times to a particular ethnic strip in the city. I became closer with them, and, eventually, we would head out on our own.

One of the doctors was a pretty suave ladies' man at the bars, much more so than the other two of us. We would meet up and find our way to different bars around the city, and not even thirty seconds after we would walk in, he would already be working it. The other doctor and I would head to the bar to get started. And at these places, which were classier than the regular bars, I would have my go-to vodka drink. But even though it was a little harder for the two of us to jump into conversations with the ladies, it didn't faze us much. The other doctor was really into the economy and the markets, and he was actually contemplating taking the most difficult financial licensing exam in the industry. So we'd have a lot to chat about.

By then I had gotten a pretty good grasp on my father's business, and all of the research had paid off. And, although I had to utilize the power of persuasion, I still didn't want to be the typical salesman. I wanted to be a straight shooter, and in fact, it would stick with me when my doctor friend called me exactly that one day. And as I began to assert my opinions about the markets to him, I got better and better at the presentation. Client meetings were much more fluid, and the words began to roll much more smoothly. I covered relevant topics with concrete ideas and professional jargon. I began to actually know what I was talking about.

So we'd hang out on the strip at a gyros joint late into the night and grab some feta cheese fries, all the while cackling about what had happened earlier that night. One night, I invited them over to my place to pre-party before we went out. They were impressed by the unit but soon began to chuckle. I still had my parents' old ripped-up white couch, and on the TV stand lay a huge stack of CDs, a small CD player/stereo, and a pencil sharpener.

"Who still has CDs?" they laughed. "And wait a minute, why the hell do you have a pencil sharpener?!"

Welcome to the digital age.

I kept going to the events every month, and I would continue to meet new and interesting people. I hit it off particularly well with a dentist couple and a tech-savvy small business owner and his wife, who was a teacher. We would all go out and have huge feasts and plenty of drink. Almost every occasion had some type of international flare or another. I would scramble to pay the checks, as is customary in my father's culture, and there would be good-natured pushback and commotion, as is also customary.

One night we were at a particularly festive ethnic restaurant, which had some highlighted entertainers. Belly dancers. I excused myself to go to the restroom, but unfortunately for me, I forgot to knock. This was a single bathroom, and a dude was on the pot. He looked up at me with a bewildered stare. I apologized, walked back to the table, and boisterously told the story to my friends. Then out came the dancers. My whole life I was under the impression that all belly dancers were women.

"Wait a minute…that's the dude!"

The scantily clad male in glittery garb thrust his hips playfully in my direction. Uncontrollable laughter. This joke would stick around for a while.

Another night we hit a different ethnic joint, where my tech friend knew the owner. We had a few bottles of the tasty customary liqueur, and things got a little cheeky from there. We closed down the restaurant, and the owner came by the table to thank us. Then the night began to pick up. As I turned my head, I caught a glimpse of the owner at the end of the table. He was gearing up to throw one of the ceramic dishes from the table. Off it went across the room onto the floor. Crash! More plates began to fly. He encouraged us to toss as well, so some of us joined in on the fun. Dinner Plate Frisbee continued until the whole restaurant floor was littered with small ceramic pieces.

I would continue to go out with my doctor friends as well, and one night we headed to a sports bar to watch a big hockey game. We came upon a table full of women and struck up a conversation. They seemed happy to talk, and things were going well—until the tall dude with the sideways hat arrived. We thought he was pretending to be one of the girls' boyfriends when he tried to inch his way into the crowded table. But one of my friends, a black belt, wasn't intimidated at all. He reached all the way up to the dude's face, pinched his cheek, and gave it a cute little tug like he would a child's, while uttering a familiar ethnic phrase for effect. The man laughed embarrassingly, and the situation was diffused.

Later that night as the bar was closing, one of the doctors and I struck up a conversation with an attractive girl—a hockey fan who was also into finance. She gave me her card, and I said I'd contact her to meet up. About a week later, we met outside at a tapas bar and enjoyed some fruity wine on a gorgeous sunny day. The conversation was smooth, and we agreed to meet up again. After a few nights out, I decided to take her to a super-fancy place that I had been wanting to go to for years. It had been the best restaurant in the city at one time or another, and this was a great opportunity to check it out. We hadn't really discussed "dating," but it still came as a surprise when she emailed me saying that she wasn't looking to date at the time. She was kind about it, and I genuinely liked her, so we kept in touch.

Around the same time, my brother's daughter was born, so my parents and I traveled out to the city where he was living to see his family. Most of my awkwardness had slowly been washed away, and family and friends out there were always gracious and welcoming. So, even though I had been quite odd for a while, things seemed to be back on track for the most part. And I don't think I skipped a beat with my sister-in-law. The more we got to know each other, the more I could see that we shared some of the same worldviews. And we got along. She never treated me as if I were awkward, even though I definitely was. And when I began talking and became more sociable again, it was as if I had always been that way.

Back home, my tech friend and our whole group went to an art fair in the city. It wasn't until that time that I really felt that I knew what kind of art I liked. I began to see things which caught my attention. I bought a few pieces and hung them up in the apartment. By that time, I had been in my condo for close to two years, and it was high time to switch things up. I ordered a new plush leather couch and chair and a fancy fifty-bottle wine cooler. As a finishing touch, I adorned the living room and the foyer with two classy chandeliers.

My tech friend also offered to help with the music situation. I agreed that something needed to be done, so he installed a state-of-the-art sound system in the condo. I could now play music in the unit with my smartphone, and I finally had a digital library of all of my CD music on hard drives. And I could access everything through a universal controller. Not to mention that I had zones. Oh, the zones. One in the living room, one in the bedroom, one in the bathroom, and one portable for either the kitchen or the balcony. And I could play different music in all of the zones *at the same time*. The party would not stop at this place.

CHAPTER ELEVEN

The Case for Empathy

ALL OF THE DRINKING and eating had taken its toll, and I had gained back basically all of the weight I had lost several years before. So I decided to join a health club. But this was not just any health club. It was more of an exclusive social club with treadmills. It was a popular spot for politicians, famous people, and rich people of all sorts. I enlisted the help of two different trainers, one for weights and one for endurance. I shot around on the basketball courts upstairs, dined at the café and the upscale restaurant, and visited the smoothie stand now and then.

But it wasn't just about the amenities at the club. I was beginning to interact with people again. All over the city. And these were quality interactions—genuine smiles, natural laughter, witty banter, and intelligent and snappy remarks. It all started to come at once. So I connected with the trainers. And the door staff at my apartment. And the guys at the bar. And the people at the golf course. That brings me to the golf course.

I had been playing at the municipal course across the street from my parents' house over the summers for close to twenty years by that time. But over the years, I usually only played with friends from high school or family. It was no doubt one of my favorite pastimes. It was somewhat liberating to be outside in the sun enjoying the fresh air and the greenery. And I could compete.

When I first picked up the game, it was all about how low I could score against others. This fire for one-upmanship had spilled over fairly easily from the academic realm to the golf course. But it wasn't only about competing against others. It was a constant quest for a personal best. I was decent at first, but as always, I knew exactly what I was doing and didn't want to take any lessons.

One year back in high school, though, my parents did send me to a golf school at a prestigious university, and I picked up some tips. But I still had some trouble listening to the instructors. I had a pretty decent hitch in my swing and some sequencing issues with the arms and the hips. One instructor jokingly coined it the "circus swing."

But over the years, the circus swing ironed out a bit, and with much practice, I did get better. And with time, I began to realize the benefits of a more calm and relaxed game, especially considering all of the internal strife that had dominated my life for so long. I didn't have the mental energy anymore to get pissed off at myself for every missed shot, which were, by the way, plentiful from time to time. Also, it looked bad and was embarrassing for family when my foul mouth and volatile temper reared their ugly heads in front of others. And lastly, I realized that it just wasn't worth it. It's just a game, it's meant for fun, and the benefits of it are numerous. And I would encounter many of those benefits that summer.

On many occasions during the season, after I'd finish what I needed to do at the office, I'd head out a little early to hit the course. Sometimes my father wouldn't be in town or wouldn't be able to play, and by that time I had fully shed the weariness of rolling out solo. So I'd jump out on the course as a single. As is customary, the starters try to group people to make foursomes. So if a group had less than four, I'd be able to join up with some other players.

And so it was that I started to meet new people—all different kinds of people. They came from various ethnic backgrounds, had unique and interesting careers, and subscribed to a myriad of diverse worldviews. But most importantly, every player had a different perspective. We chatted about all sorts of things, including life, family, entertainment, and the subtleties of the game. But what began to pop out at me was not just that each of us lives in different realities and thus forms different viewpoints. Actually, it was much of the opposite.

I began to notice the extent of our common nature and shared incentives as human beings. Once you wade through all of the superficiality, persona, and veneer, you begin to realize that most people want the same things out of life. It's not money or pleasure or notoriety that really drives us. That's not who we really are as a species.

The way I see it, we all have a genetic makeup designed for evolutionary success. The most important element of our existence is survival. If we don't survive, we go extinct. So in that vein, our bodies and minds are in a constant struggle with our environment to adapt to changing circumstances to extend our life cycles.

But the survival of the self only makes sense if it lasts in perpetuity, because if it didn't, the eventual inevitability of death would lead to extinction as well. So, of course, the built-in mechanism for that is the undying desire to spread the seed of life, to foster its growth, and to protect it from harm and death. Until, of course, that individual can procreate as well to continue the chain of being. Those ingrained desires are therefore not just designed for the preservation of self, but also, and more importantly, for the species that it helps to perpetuate. So in essence, we are all hardwired the same way for a common purpose. This root commonality is at the heart of what it means to be alive.

Now, it is also true that the desire to procreate initiates a driving force to find the healthiest and most qualified mate to aid in passing along the best genes for the greatest chance at survival of the progeny. And it is also true that this driving force leads to competition among members of the same species, both for attracting the best mate and for garnering enough resources to protect and foster the growth of their young. However, all this being true, I would posit that we now, at this moment in our development, have a much cleaner and smoother pathway to survival.

Specifically, as human beings, we have the capability of utilizing cognitive thought at a level not known to any other species on this Earth, as far as we know, that is. And in that sense, because we have reached a level of consciousness amenable to elevated, rational, and logical thought, we now have the skills necessary for creative idea generation and complex problem-solving.

With these gifts, we have developed a much deeper understanding of both our internal and external environments. And with our current level of understanding of the world we live in, we have the ability to coordinate our efforts to allocate our resources efficiently so that survival of both the individual and the species essentially becomes a foregone conclusion. Our ancient adversarial paradigm thus becomes effectively obsolete. It can now be seen as not only an unnecessary course of action, but a largely unproductive one as well. Although our ingrained genetic desires still remain, we now have the ability to adjust our conduct to utilize our commonalities to survive, rather than to exploit our differences for the same goal. This is adaptation, and this is evolution.

So when we attempt to see each other as similar beings, with similar emotions and cognition, and designed for a similar purpose, we are staring directly into the looking glass of the evolution of humanity. This is how we are able to connect. It is why we talk about our families to each other. It is why we express our deepest hopes and wishes in the same manner. What is most important in our lives? Biologically *and* intellectually, we all inevitably come up with the same answer.

And as I began to meet more and more people on the golf course, I started to see this more and more clearly—especially when I was fortuitously paired up with two particular brothers. They were both considerably older than me and had grown up far across the seas. But the moment we shook hands, I could sense the humanity in them. They took kind to a different place—a higher, more elevated plateau. They offered me trail mix treats and granola bars. We chatted about family, careers, and all things uplifting. It was mostly lighthearted banter at first. But we would later exchange numbers, and I would be seeing a lot of them on the golf course from then on.

Back in the city, I continued to go out at night and thirst for social interaction of any kind. I began to talk to people more and more at the neighborhood bar. The pool table was a good way to start a fluid conversation, and I would spend most of my time there. I snatched up some of my old high school swagger and college mojo from off the shelf. I talked to everyone who crossed my path. These were people from all elements of society. It was much different than the golf course, though. These were mostly younger people. They were more energized, and they often came from different socioeconomic strata. I soaked that in. Stigma, prejudice, presumption, and assumption popped out at me, and I swept them cleanly off my shoulder. I was a student, and this was my classroom. I listened, and I learned.

It was clear to me that all of these people wanted the same things out of life as the people on the golf course. They were compassionate, sensitive, caring, and intelligent. And they could express themselves articulately, sometimes in many different languages. And they had heart. A whole lot of it. All you had to do was give them a chance. Some might have appeared menacing, or even dangerous at first, but when they cracked a smile and you found it in their eyes, you could see the true human being and not just his or her form. I found this to be a veritable phenomenon—one that had been collecting dust, one that was known but easily dismissed, understood but often forgotten. I kept learning.

On the drives around the city, I'd talk to all of the cab drivers. Most of them were from a particular continent, and I began to pick up the nuances in their accents. I'd pull the "Let-me-guess-where-you're-from" routine, and it would work—and well at that. Ice shattered, we'd get on a roll. In a five-minute cab ride, we would cover some of the best highlights of the human condition. These guys knew exactly what I was talking about. And I understood them. I'm sure that many of them weren't used to chatterbox passengers waxing poetic on the meaning of life, but we connected. We really connected. We laughed so much on one ride that one man even called me a "happy factory." I was beginning to understand.

My personal desires did not desist, though. Even though I'd have fun out and about in the city, I was still terribly alone. Some of it was probably due to the content of the conversations themselves. As I saw and understood more and more, I began to realize exactly what I had been missing. I would hit the strip clubs often, and at home, the girls would come and go as they always did. The drink would inevitably do its trick, most of the time at the wee hours of the morning. I would satisfy my desires for a day or two, but they would come back even stronger the next time. It was a ferocious hunger, and I was always starving. It happened again and again and again—an unending stream, a revolving door of sorts. Some were familiar, some were new and exciting, and some elite. But it was never just the typical lascivious wham-bam for me. These were also intense study sessions. No joke.

I was a host. I would greet them with a warm hug and a smile and offer them wine or champagne, sometimes some of my best stuff. We'd toast and just talk for a while. I met some super-interesting people that way. We'd talk about many of the same things as I did with the folks on the golf course, in the bars, and in the cabs. These were good people. They were human beings. And we also connected.

One night back at the bar, I was strutting around the pool table, and I was on fire. I had the feeling. In one particular game, the force was strong. I walked up to a ball without even lining it up, knocked it in, and rolled on to the next one—until I cleared the entire table. Just after I finished, I struck up a conversation with a young dude that was in the area, and we got along right off the bat. But there were so many people, so many cards, so many numbers, that I would start to lose track. Especially with the drink. The faces would all blur together, and I'd just toss all of the business cards on my desk in a big pile. I wouldn't think too much of this interaction until the next time I saw him.

One day I walked into the bar, and he was the first one I saw. He turned around, saw me, and jumped off his stool to greet me. We chatted for a while, and he told me that he worked in film and television production for a major sports franchise in the city. We both decided that the night was young. The night was always young. So we hit a club. And then another club. We would soon be doing the circuit frequently. And this was no "waiting-in-line-for-an-hour-just-to-grind-like-sardines-on-a-messy-dance-floor" kind of a thing. We did it up right. I'd walk straight up to the bouncer in the suit with the earpiece and the clipboard. I'd assess the situation and make things happen. The confidence. The swagger. People responded to it. They respected it. And the twenties. The bouncers, the promoters, the bartenders, and the muscle security—they all got a healthy dose of the paper.

We would be ushered to the corner tables, past all of the commotion, sometimes the special back way through the kitchen. Then the bottles would pop. First the champagne, then the vodka. The sexy waitresses wearing skintight clothes, and not much of it, would do the honors. Sometimes the champagne was adorned with obnoxious sparklers for the whole club to see, and the vodka was always accompanied by colorful mixers. Bumping music reverberated throughout the dimly lit VIP areas—techno, dance, club, pop—anything to get the crowd moving. Made-up girls in tight dresses gyrated everywhere—at the table, on the table, everywhere. One go-to club even had the "throne," as my new friend coined it—a single seat in the back corner of the club adjacent to one of the best tables. We would grace that throne a lot over the next year or so.

It became so easy. I'd just hit up the promoter, he'd have his guy waiting at the door for me, and we'd get to business. We'd party until closing time. But when the lights came on, it was time to settle. And the good stuff at the clubs wasn't in the same ballpark as the bottles in the store. They came with sparklers after all. And a few nights a week would require backing. So the withdrawals from the account continued.

I would hang out with my new friend regularly from then on. We would become closer over time. He also introduced me to his circle of friends, and although they were considerably younger than I was, their age didn't even come to mind much. I was making up for lost time So we'd hit the ballgames, the bars, and the clubs. It was a fabulous blur. I would make my entrances into the establishments and do the usual rounds of hand slapping, fist bumps, and hugs. So much so that my friend once called me "The Mayor."

One weekend my uncle from overseas came into town, and I decided to show him a good time. We hopped into the stretch limo at my parents' house in the 'burbs, downtown or bust. My uncle was much younger than my father, but still up there in years, though you couldn't really tell with his mindset. He was one of us. And he was suave. The suavest. He had the charm, the mojo, the stuff. So when he saw what I had gotten into, he seemed pretty surprised, to say the least. My family, especially my parents, was pretty much unawares, mostly because I didn't tell them much. I was the same person with them as I was in the city, but I think it was hard for them to see sometimes. I had the same perspective and attitude and was able to make the same connections with people, but I think the past got in the way much of the time.

My uncle saw it, though. He understood. And it wasn't just the nonsense and the superficiality of much of the atmosphere either. In fact, I wouldn't even talk to many of the girls at the clubs. I'd spend more time sometimes talking about life and relationships with the waitresses. That was reality. The rest was just a pastime, a diversion, an escape of sorts. And I knew that. I would talk about all of these things with my uncle. We would have deep conversations about positivity, respect, peace, and social betterment. We connected.

By that time, I had had a new doctor for my medication for about a year or so, and things were going well. He came in right at the upswing, and we were able to link up from the beginning. I divulged much more to this doctor. But I was still embarrassed and ashamed at the revolving door of girls and the extent of the drinking, so I kept some of that close to home. But we did have many honest conversations about my condition. He was an intelligent man, and I enjoyed pondering the limits and recesses of known psychology with him, especially as it related to my me and my experience. I followed his thoughts and he mine. I would be able to hang on to his ideas and answer sometimes-complex questions with logical and substantive analysis, as I saw it at least. I expressed myself, and he had some profound questions that drove at the heart of some of my own thoughts and beliefs, both in this reality and in the subtextual code world. I learned.

I would explain to the doctor my consternation at losing the sense of self and my surroundings that I had remembered from growing up and before my first incident in college. Although the memories were distant and fading, I tried to describe the zest for life and the feeling of being that had disappeared when I was introduced to the round pink pill so many years before. He listened to me intently and understood what I was saying by terming it "smelling the flowers." So the doctor soon consolidated my medication. I would now take only the small pink pill and a flaky white pill. Over time, and as things continued to progress, the doses of each would be cut in half. Thus, the small pink pill would eventually transform into a small blue one.

Back at the office, I had finished the designation program and the two months of self-study. Soon after, I sat for the ten-hour, two-day exam. I had regained my confidence, the words made sense, the math certainly made sense, and I understood the questions. I finished early.

Around that time, we had another small shakeup in the office. Our more senior assistant decided to take a new position elsewhere in the office, and we were once again on the hunt for a new one. Luckily, we found an experienced and dedicated woman who was available at the time. Actually, we had known her from the transition, as she had been in a branch office position back then. She had been able to help us out immensely with the operations aspect of our move. I was involved in the hiring negotiations with her, and we started off on the right foot. She was professional and hard working, and it seemed like the team was finally coming together a bit.

But some of the remnants of the old situation still remained with our other assistant. She was so kind, but over time she developed an unwillingness to take any direction. She became somewhat disagreeable at times and constantly pushed back on my opinions, assertions, and professional judgment. I knew I had to be a boss, but I didn't want to be bossy. And I would waver on this one painfully. I truly empathized with her. I could see her crying at her desk during the day. Everyone could. She was constantly wiping her eyes. It became a regular thing.

I don't know how much of it had to do with our team, but when I asked her into my office to talk, she assured me that it didn't have anything to do with me. What hit me the hardest, though, was that I knew how that felt. I was torn. I wanted to show her compassion and kindness, but we had to have a professional work environment and get our job done as well. We weren't functioning optimally, and we had a responsibility to my father and our clients. I was in knots.

Around the same time, I decided to throw a holiday party. Not many of the folks in my extended family had gotten a chance to see my new-look apartment, so I thought it'd be fun to have them over. We had a pretty decent turnout—my mother's brother's family, my mother's cousin and his family, and my parents. It was pretty much a packed house. I made sure that the zones were in full effect with a premade playlist, that the wine and champagne were flowing, and that the treats were plentiful. Nothing was really said about my awkward behavior in the past. We talked, laughed, and got along pretty much as if the previous decade had almost never even transpired.

I remember one night in particular before that party as well. I met up with a cousin on my mother's side who I hadn't seen in a while. She had been out with her friends that night, and I had been out and about as well. So I thought I'd take them to a piano bar down the street from my condo and pop a bottle of bubbly with them. She seemed to be quite taken aback when she saw me grease the door staff and the manager to get the best table up front. We had a blast, and sometime that night she gave me a big hug and let out an even bigger sigh of relief. I could tell that she was happy to see me back.

The next week I had another party to throw. It was actually billed as one of those networking functions through my friend's organization, and this time I was the host. I had won a bidding auction through a charity for an open party at a restaurant/bar, and I thought it would be a perfect venue to have the gathering. I fretted a little about organizing and logistics but still managed to make it happen. The usual crowd was there, and we did our thing, as always. But I did see someone else there I hadn't seen in forever.

She was the sister of a boy I went to grade school and junior high with. The boy had had some troubles, and the kids would pick on him mercilessly. One day I was with a friend who lived next door to him, and my friend ran into his yard doing laps in the grass. I parted the bushes to see what was happening and decided to walk through the brush into the yard. When the boy ran out screaming to protect his property, I wasn't sure exactly what to do. I kind of froze as he ran toward me. I just stood there as he tried to wrestle me. I didn't want any part of a fight.

In fact, from what I can remember, I had never picked a fight in my life, except with my brother of course. So when he grappled with me, I was a little taken aback. He swept my leg and I started to fall. My left arm slipped under my side as I went down, and my hipbone landed square over the middle of my forearm. Crack! I could hear it break, and when I looked at it, it was deformed and mangled. I dragged myself to my friend's yard and pulled myself up onto a stone ledge next to a garden on the side of his house. The marrow hit the bloodstream. I almost passed out.

The doctor tried to set the bone, but it wouldn't really take that well, and I was in more pain than I had ever felt before. Pretty much right after I got out of the cast, I fell again, this time running out of gym class down the stairs. It was a compound fracture in almost exactly the same place. I didn't make as much of an effort as I should have on the physical therapy, so I would have to live with a little bevel in my arm. I still favor it to this day. Sometimes I even wake up in the middle of the night nervous that I might have unknowingly broken it rolling over or something.

But what I really regret is what happened after that at school. I had gained some popularity as being smart at first, and then by running around with the "cool" kids. It's not to say that these kids were all mean by any stretch, though, and many of them were actually genuine people and good friends. But this poor guy was still constantly harassed. So when the rumors started to circulate about the incident, he obviously ended up on the losing end of the telephone game. He was seen as attacking me from behind, and although he did come at me first, I didn't do enough to dispel the inaccuracy. What I didn't fully understand was the cultural shame and stigma that comes from blindsiding someone. It's seen as a cowardly act, one for weaker aggressors. It's playing dirty, and I should have known that.

So to say the least, I was surprised to see his sister at the party that night. She had just moved into town from another city and had met up with my friend who ran the organization. We hadn't known each other very well back home, but we got to talking and caught up. By the end of the night, we exchanged numbers.

A few days later, I had another shindig at the condo, this time for friends. Another good turnout featured my tech friend and his wife, my dentist friends, my old networking friend, and a few others. We picked at a gingerbread house centerpiece, sipped on some great wine, enjoyed a few chill tunes, unwrapped some fantastic birthday gifts, and topped off the night with a delicious chocolate birthday cake. We would get together again several times—at hookah joints, at the dentists' place in the suburbs, and for a special New Year's Eve party at my tech friend and his wife's apartment in the city. We danced to silly music, puffed on double apple, and I donned a cowboy hat and crooned for a giggling audience. And I had some particularly thoughtful conversations with my dentist friend. We delved deep into philosophy, psychology, ethics and morality, social progression, and life betterment.

I also began to visit my parents' place at the coast as they spent more and more time there. I soon found out that many of the families from my high school had also bought vacation places down there. One in particular was the family of a friend who I had gone to school and played Little League with way back when. He was actually the friend I had met up with on the golf course right after my incident in college. He had seen me with the headphones and already knew the deal. So when we got in touch and met up out there, I could see that he noticed the change in me right away. In fact, he gave me a hug that was almost identical to the one that my cousin had given me not long before. I would try to meet up with him whenever we were both at the coast from then on.

Back home, I continued to go to the networking functions every month. One night I struck up a conversation with a guy who I had seen a few times before but hadn't had the chance to meet. He told me he was a neurosurgeon, and I laughed. He looked younger than me, and I could tell that he had party-boy mode as well. But it turned out that he really was serious about his profession. We exchanged numbers and planned to meet up sometime in the city.

He was a built and attractive guy, and the ladies certainly took a liking to him. He was always plugged in. Every time we went out, groups of people from here and there would come out of the woodwork. We'd be at a bar or a club, and women from all over would stop by and talk to us. He knew some, but not others. He had a certain charm, and he knew how to disarm a woman's defenses easily. For his uncanny ability to gather people, especially women, into one place, my friend from the sports franchise dubbed him "The Sweeper." The Sweeper and I would become friends and would end up hanging out a lot that year.

One night when we were on our way to a club, my friend from the sports franchise asked if we could stop by and pick up his sister. The cab rolled up, and we jumped out to heavy flakes. I could barely make out the image of a girl under the glare of some streetlights. She was waving to him excitedly from the dusted white sidewalk. She trekked through the thick powder, and we all hopped into a cab en route to the club. We partied for a while, she went home early, and we stayed late as usual.

Soon after, that same friend invited me to see a production his sister was performing in. She was outstanding. But it wasn't until later that I would realize that her depth wasn't just reserved to her acting on stage. We met her after the show, and we made our way back to my apartment, where a friend of hers joined us. We chatted for a while over a glass of wine, and before she left, she gave me her email address. It wouldn't be long before I would contact her.

I also continued hang out with the sister of the boy with whom I had had that run-in in junior high. Since I wasn't dating anyone, I think she saw me as a "project" of sorts. She said my power suits and banker hairstyle made me look too old. So we went shopping together. We rolled around the department store for a while, but I wasn't too into the whole operation. She picked out almost all of the clothes, and we eventually pushed the cart up to the counter, a hefty bundle of trendy threads inside.

Then we went to the salon to get me coiffed. I went out once wearing the clothes and sporting the new hairstyle, but when my dentist friend called me "2.0" like a software program, I knew that something wasn't right. As I was still pretty chunky, the clothes were too tight and felt pretty uncomfortable. So I stopped wearing them. When she found out, she was not happy to say the least. I think she felt that I misled her in some way. We wouldn't really see much of each other after that.

I would continue to see someone who she introduced me to, though. We were at a popular bar when she brought a girl over to meet me. She was blonde and attractive, and we seemed to get along. We would end up going out a few times, and I invited her to my place to watch a big game on TV one weekend. I put out several huge dishes of chips and salsa, breads and cheeses, deserts, and all sorts of other stuff. But that night it was only the two of us. Overdoing it was an understatement. She kindly helped wash all of the dishes, but I think we both knew at the time that it probably wasn't going to work. We tried to reconnect a few times, but we lost touch pretty quickly after that as well.

Back to the money. I had not only been using the funds from the account with my mother's and my name on it, but I had been using one of my parents' credit cards as well. I usually reserved it for meals, drinks, and incidentals. I tried my best to keep it just to that so as not to sound any alarm bells. But one day I was out at a strip club, once again solo, and they wouldn't take my personal credit card for some reason.

I didn't have enough cash on me and had maxed out my ATM allotment from the bank for the day. I had no choice. I hoped that my parents wouldn't see the charge, but my mother was nothing but meticulous with the credit card statements. She noticed the expense as something unusual and did some digging. Although the name of the club was coded as something innocuous, I heard later that she managed to find a lascivious website connected to the establishment.

It was around the same time that my father also noticed that the joint account had been decimated to half of its original value and that my own accounts had been dwindling as well. So off we went to see both my therapist and my medication doctor. My therapist was also an MD, and they both immediately recognized the runaway spending as a common issue for people with my particular diagnosis. My medication doctor adjusted the dosages of my pills a bit, and I would attempt to tighten the belt over the next month. I was able to produce decent results, relatively speaking, but, as they say all too often, old habits die hard.

Fortunately (or unfortunately, depending how you look at it) for me, the firm soon came out with a new incentive program. They would offer their employees a forgivable loan in the amount of a certain percentage of production. A portion of that debt would be wiped off the books every year, until the last year of the loan term, when the employee would be free and clear. The only sticking point was the contract term. If I took the loan, I would have to be with the firm for several more years, or else I'd have to repay the unforgiven portion back to the firm. I didn't even think twice. So, having that cash plus a decent-sized liquid investment account as a kitty, I found a way to feed my habits, at least for the time being.

The next month I had a big trip planned. My aunt on my father's side had been looking at charity auctions on the internet and had come across some vacation prizes for donations to the organization. She bid on one of their trips and won a cruise for two to an island across the ocean. The plan was to circumnavigate this island in a small ship and stop at points of interest all along the way. We decided to go together.

Since I would be traveling a bit before my aunt would get there, I flew out alone to the capital city of a country just off the coast from the island. The country had always been known around the world for its ancient civilization, and I enjoyed touring around for a few days. I had been there in college, but I got a much richer taste of it this time, if only for a short while. I had a guide for a full day and was able to hit some major tourist destinations. I was then off to a small island nation to board the cruise ship.

I met my aunt there, and we toured the island for a day before the trip. I hadn't seen her in a while, although we still were talking on the phone quite frequently. So it was good to catch up in person. We had a banquet dinner and some introductions before embarking the next day. We would find out over the next week and a half or so that many of the people were cultured, traveled, and educated. So the conversations at meals and on the excursions were often substantive. It was an older crowd, but I never really felt too out of place. The staff was welcoming and professional, and we packed a lot into those ten days or so.

As we pushed off for the trip around the larger island nation, some of the old concepts began to swirl a bit. I gradually began to pick up meaning in things again. I would entertain these thoughts, and they would soon begin to snowball. Significant and synchronous events began to pop frequently, and things were coming back to me. Although this subtextual code-world had never fully left my consciousness, I could sense the connections beginning to form freely once again in the front of my mind.

But this time was even more refined than the last. The familiar whispering returned and became louder as the trip progressed. And the images began to appear here and there as well. However, the constant internal bickering had been muted considerably. In fact, I felt able to return the whispers and the images in my head without too much pushback. When I did hear some banging, consistent beeping, or other noises, it did register. But I felt much more capable to deal with it this time. I'd often simply flash back a smiley face, a peace sign, or other various symbols in an array of different colors. I'd even post written messages across my vision, and it would seem to work.

Regardless of the internal chatter, though, I still participated in the group activities that the travel guides had organized. We toured ancient ruins, visited wineries, passed by olive fields, strolled through quaint villages, and hiked up an active volcano. As the trip progressed, however, themes began to weave into all of the activities. Everything around me was part of a grander story, and I was the central character—the protagonist if you will. I donned my headphones once again on the ship, on the buses, through the streets, and even on some of the guided walking tours. When we visited some of the magnificently built and designed churches and cathedrals, I would try to suppress the whispering out of respect. But the snap negatives were not gone altogether. In fact, on one occasion a particularly profane anti-religious comment came crashing in as loud as a thought can be, with full text across my vision. I swiveled and hit the exit immediately.

Religion would continue to be a conceptual thread throughout the trip. For me, it pertained mostly to attempting to resolve the differences among the major religions by focusing on their commonalities. The difficult part, however, was attempting to reconcile the particular narratives. I continued to try, with reason and logic, the best I could in the midst of the flashing images, synchronous stimuli, and whispering thoughts. There were times when I felt as if I were overheating, but I tried some "Zen" mind techniques—an attempt at self-taught meditation of sorts. Sometimes this worked and sometimes not, but I was continuing to sharpen the toolset and was intent on further honing the skills.

I noticed that some of the most difficult stretches involved projecting the body signals, the whispering, and the images onto other people. This was a tricky one. Many of the folks in the group or on the street were at times crossing their arms, itching body parts, and speaking in sync with my music or the environment around them. But when I attributed, let's say anger, to a gentleman who crossed his arms, the negativity would increase, and I'd begin to overheat.

I somehow knew that this phenomenon was larger than direct signals from these folks to me, but it was difficult to separate the actor from the action. I could sense that their brains were involved, simply because they were active. Their neurons were firing as they spoke, gesticulated, and displayed body signals, just like mine were.

"But are they conscious of it?" I thought to myself. "Or are they unconsciously communicating? Or is someone or something communicating for or through them?"

It would take a while for me to refine this concept, and I wouldn't fully tackle it on this trip.

After we disembarked onto the small island where we began the voyage, I took a short flight to visit my uncle in a country not too far away. As the external stimuli had died down in intensity, so had the racing thoughts. I was planning on staying for a few more days when I suddenly got an email from one of my assistants at the office and a follow-up call from my father. Her email was a lengthy message about our activities in the office. It read somewhat like she was putting things on record, almost as if for a legal document. Aside from the general tone, though, a particular portion of the letter caught my attention. I interpreted it as an insinuation that some of the issues in the office were due to my neglect or lack of leadership in some way.

I tried to Zen again, but I couldn't help but take some offense to those words. Maybe I read too much into it. Maybe she was simply unhappy with the work environment, and that was her way of letting us know in a professional manner. I couldn't be sure, but the tone of the letter still left a lingering sour feeling within me.

My father suggested that I come home to deal with the issue, and I agreed. By that time, I had found out that I had passed the designation examination for the financial license. And I had also been deeply involved in many of the client meetings and communications. I was also managing a test portfolio of my own, and I was beginning to serve as the point person for daily office adviser duties when my father was away. I was a professional now, and I had to accept the responsibility that comes with that label. So I flew home the next day to assess the situation.

Things continued to devolve with our assistant, especially the eroding relationship between her and my father, and now also between her and the other assistant. I began to work more closely with the other assistant as well, and gave less and less work to the first one as time went on. I didn't know what else to do at that point. I still felt torn. The crying at her desk got worse, and I didn't feel ethically that it was my place to try to ask her about her personal issues. If I had known her outside of the office, it would be a no-brainer. I would try to offer her assistance. I would try to help console her any way I could. I would lend her a hand in some way. But here I felt as if my hands were tied. I did let her know on one particular occasion that she could talk to me about anything she wanted and that my office was an open door for her. But that's about all I felt I could do at the time. There was no easy solution. I had some more thinking to do.

CHAPTER TWELVE

Old Ball, New Game

OUTSIDE THE OFFICE, I continued my parade around town. I strutted around the city and the clubs with my friend from the sports franchise. We jumped into random limos and black cars on the street, I sifted my way through long lines of antsy partygoers, and I continued to toss twenties this way and that. But my friend had some pull as well. His young age didn't prevent him from establishing a solid career and gaining professional traction pretty much immediately. He invited me to a bunch of games way up in the private skyboxes, and he introduced me to some interesting folks at the organization. Better yet, he knew the players. I got to meet several of the guys, and I would see them out in the city from time to time. Eventually, a few of them even began to frequent our tables at the clubs.

One night we closed down one of our go-to clubs, I paid the check, and I saw my friend off in a cab. It was early in the morning, and I found myself on the street alone thinking about my next move. Just then, the exit doors to the club swung open, and out came a big-time player we had been hanging out with that night. Without the thumping music, we could finally hear each other, and we got to chatting. He was young, but he seemed like an authentic and genuine guy. In fact, many of the guys from that team seemed to share those qualities. I feel like a lot of athletes get a reputation for being flashy prima donnas who make it a practice to be rude and obnoxious to others, but this guy seemed different. In any case, we hung out for a while, he tossed me his digits, and off he went in a cab.

Soon after, our team was gearing up for a huge series with another dominating team filled with superstars. The games would be held in a city on the coast, which was well known for its late-night parties. My friend suggested that I come down for the full playoff experience. I agreed without much hesitation at all, booked a room at the same hotel the players were staying at, and hopped on a plane out there. I met up with the friend I had seen at my parents' place on the other coast of that same state, and we drove out to the city together.

Once there, we went up to the counter to check in. Just as we were walking to the elevator, we bumped into the campaign manager for the most well-known politician in the world. He happened to be from my city, and we chatted for a quick minute about the team and the game in the elevator.

I asked him if he was going to the game, and he answered in the affirmative, adding, "Strength in numbers."

I laughed as we came to our floor and got off the elevator.

As I made my way downstairs again to meet my friend who worked for the team, it was as if I were inside my television set. I soaked in all of the personalities—sports broadcasters and analysts, coaches, former superstar players from back in the day, current superstar athletes. The place was a veritable la-la land. As I strolled out to the pool area, I bumped into the player I had exchanged numbers with at the club. We chatted for a second before I met up with my friend for a fruity cocktail and a fancy steak burger.

That night, we decided to find a party. We met up with one of the team trainers my friend had introduced me to a while before. I had been hanging out with this dude in the city as well, and we would often go to the clubs together as a group. He made a quick call, and one of the players came down to meet us. The concierge flagged down a cab for us, and even though it was a mini-van, I'm not sure how this guy's bulky seven-foot frame fit in. But he managed, and off we went. It was a foregone conclusion that bottle service would be in order that night. We would hit several clubs over our time in the city, and I would go to both games. Although our team ended up losing both, I felt satisfied that my mark had been made.

Back home, I had by then already contacted my friend's sister. We decided to meet up, and she suggested we hit a happy hour. I was game, so I picked a trendy bar in the city where we could get together. We had a few appetizers and chatted for a while. Then came the cocktails. We decided to be adventurous and try some of their creatively named signature drinks. It was happy hour after all. We had a few, and I ended up having a blast. We connected pretty quickly. She was easy to talk to and had a sunny personality. She was much younger than me, but she was definitely with it. I enjoyed talking to her.

I emailed her fairly soon after to ask her out again, and she got back to me right away. She agreed to go out, but she mentioned that she had just begun to see someone more seriously and that she wasn't looking to date. I said I understood, but I thought it would still be good to get to know each other better. We would continue to go out every so often to the happy hours and have a few drinks. We made it a ritual to try the signature cocktails, and we would always get a kick out of their quirky names.

Happy hours turned into dinners, and I began to ask her if she wanted to continue the night. Each time she would politely decline, and we'd go our separate ways until the next time. After a few more happy hours, she wrote me another email. She reiterated that she wasn't looking to date but that she still enjoyed my company and wanted to continue our friendship and get-togethers.

I was conflicted. Even though she was considerably younger, she was still super mature for her age. I liked her a lot, and it seemed like we connected really well. I guess I was interested in her, but I had to respect that she was dating someone. I was put in a tough position. All of the clubbing and the fast life got me going, and I was definitely having fun. But it was exhausting, and deep down I knew that I wanted something different. And I was still alone. I was so damn alone.

So we continued to see each other every so often, but in the back of my mind I always knew that I would feel horrible if I let my selfishness get the best of me by trying to push the envelope. Plus, I didn't know if my friend knew about how much I was seeing his sister. Although I told him that I had met up with her, I didn't tell him much else. And I didn't want to put a strain on our friendship either, since he had become one of the closest friends I had had over the past year—actually in a long, long time.

So, although I was being dragged in two different directions, I knew what the right answer was. I eventually had to pull back a little and give her some space. Over time, I would try to reel in the flirtatiousness and just keep our meetings to good friends catching up. It would take time, but eventually it would settle in like that. It was the right thing to do.

Soon after, I had a big college reunion coming up, and I was excited to see old friends. I had only seen a few of my closer friends now and then over the previous decade, but I knew that they and many other college buddies would be there. I wasn't too nervous that people knew about what had happened so many years before. A lot of time had passed, and things were much different by then. I figured that they would be able to grasp that.

I flew in to the familiar little airport, expectations on high. And I rode into town in style. I reserved a black car from the airport and had a great chat with the driver over the hour-and-a-half drive. By then I had been accustomed to infusing positivity, understanding, tolerance, and the dignity of all human beings into most of my conversations. And I was getting much better at explaining the logic and rationale for most of my thought processes.

Almost every conversation would be a continuous stream of agreement and cognitive synergies. I was on the same page as other people—almost always. I knew without a doubt that I was onto something. Almost everyone knows these things. Almost everyone believes these things. But not everyone articulates them. And many times people neglect to think about them. I mean *really* think about them. We get so wrapped up in our daily lives that we often forget to stop and think sometimes. So much noise, so much confusion, so little harmony. There was a space for this discussion. There was a need for it. And I knew it.

I was determined not to fall into the old habits I had developed in college so many years before. I would branch out, meet new people, and connect with ones who I might not have paid as much attention to in the past. I wouldn't just follow the crowd and get stuck in the basement with the beer all day. I was over all of that. My life had changed—for the better.

Things started well. I met up with an old acquaintance and his wife. We had been in some of the same circles in college, and I knew that he was a really good dude, but I hadn't gotten to know him much. We hung out and played a little pong—just the three of us for a while. I had a blast. It was how college should have been. We were laughing. About good things. Not derisive, negative garbage. We were just living.

I also met some new people. They were different than me. They were really smart and interesting. They had gone on to pursue socially productive and intellectually stimulating careers. I continued to venture out on my own to planned activities I used to pass over in a heartbeat. I must have missed so many rich and worthwhile experiences at that school. It was a magnificent place to study, but I had tossed much of that in with the garbage I used to so mindlessly toss down the stairs of the dorms.

I also reconnected with a few folks from my fraternity. I had been a part of some rocky scenes with some of them, but much of that was water under the bridge by then. We played pong outside, and I felt good. At one point I saw one of our brothers walking out of the fraternity house, and I felt I had to stop him as he passed by. I had been a jackass, especially to him, over our time at the house.

He was a really nice kid, but he got picked on a lot, sometimes because of his weight. The older kids would throw out a nickname that he used to hate, and I used to jump in. I replayed it in my mind.

"What the holy hell was I thinking? I had had the same awful shit done to me in high school, and I knew exactly how that felt. And I turned around and did the same thing to this poor guy?! What an asshole I was!"

But throughout those years I spent in the darkness, I feel like I found the answer to that question. It came from introspection—that brutal honesty that I threw at myself, all alone in my desolate apartment, amidst all of that banging on the walls. I felt it. I could sense the cycle of violence, abuse, and neglect. I could see how that passes on from person to person, generation to generation, in perpetuity. I understood this vicious loop.

I could see the contagion, the network of negativity that spreads from one interaction all the way down the chain of causation. I could see how that tears at the fabric of society. And how it slowly eats away at a person's spirit. I knew the destructiveness that lay squarely on that side of the coin. I had to break that cycle, in the present, in the now.

So I put my arm around my fraternity brother and apologized. I just apologized. It was all I could do at that point.

I'm not sure how he felt, especially because this was over a decade too late. He uncomfortably tossed me a quick, "No worries," as if he wasn't exactly sure what I was talking about. He then turned around and made his way across the lawn. And as I saw him head up the sidewalk and out of view, I thought to myself that it was good to see that he had, in fact, moved on.

The next stop was to a different fraternity to say hello to a few people, and I ran into three of my best friends from back in the day. Actually, they were the ones who had prevented my limp body from hitting the ground in the parking lot way back when. One of them, after hearing my new philosophy on life earlier that day, cynically called me "Mr. Positive." I responded by saying that I didn't see the point in being negative. If we have a choice as to how we think and act, if we really do have that capability, then why choose the negative? Why do that? What does that accomplish? Logically, what is the productivity in that, and who does that benefit? And alternatively, look at the other side and the synergies that arise from positive thought and genuine and sincere connections with others. It couldn't be clearer to me.

I think it was still pretty hard for some of them to believe.

One friend even said, "But I *know* you."

As if the actions of that selfish, rude bastard I used to be were simply the results of a genetic personality trait. I refuse to believe that. People can change. And they do. And more importantly, people can find out who they really are—if they choose to look hard enough, that is. Sometimes it's difficult. Sometimes it's even an earth-shattering proposition. I know that very well. But what I also know is that that immaturity, that act that I had so stupidly carried over from high school for those two or three years in college, that was *not* me.

I also got in a few rounds of golf on the campus course. It seemed much more peaceful playing there this time. It wasn't at all like that hectic mushroom trip I took in college, where we tumbled down the hill of the fifth hole doing somersaults. Wow, was that a bad experience. The mushrooms had been stolen from a friend earlier that night, and I wasn't very comfortable with that whole operation. By the time I stumbled home that night, filthy and covered with mud, I was spent, emotionally and physically. I'm not even sure how I made it home, but after I saw our fraternity dogs' faces morph, I made a beeline for my bed, curled up, and began shaking.

But those times were long gone, and I strolled down the main street enjoying the sun. I grabbed a bite to eat at one of the restaurants on campus that I rarely ventured out to in college and did some window-shopping. I dipped into one of the college memorabilia shops and decided that I needed a few things. I had never really been as proud of the college as I should have been.

I knew that I hadn't taken advantage of all of the incredible things it had to offer, but I still felt that I had gotten a great education. I still went to classes enough to know that the professors were excellent and that higher-level thought was going on inside me, whether I liked it or not. The beers certainly didn't drown all of that away. And I shared some good experiences with some good friends. So I bought some clothes and things. I would begin to wear them from then on. Proudly.

After the reunion, I flew to a coastal resort where our firm was hosting its annual conference for the top producers in the country. My father would bring me along as his guest, and I was happy to go. I got some golf in, we had some good conversations over dinner, and I got to meet some of the top brass. In fact, the big boss who my father had interviewed with so long before at the big-bucks firm had now become the head of our firm. I ran into him after one of their meetings, and he kindly smiled and shook my hand.

I smiled back amidst all of the flashing lights and clicking cameras around us. He would eventually send me one of the pictures of us shaking hands with a note saying that it was good to see me at the resort. I found it somewhat surprising that he would write to me. But it was certainly a good kind of surprising. I think I still have that picture somewhere.

When I got home, I decided that it was time to recapture some of the glory days. I used to love playing baseball as a kid. I would get amped up all day at school for every game and would play my heart out on the field. It was fun to be part of a team. I was a pretty decent player and would make most of the Little League all-star teams. I played up to my early teens, but I didn't try out for the team in high school. I always kind of regretted that.

But I wouldn't anymore. I joined an adult baseball league way out in the boonie suburbs. It was hilarious. I wasn't really as good as I had thought. Plus, my body was getting old, and it didn't respond so well to the dives and the slides any more. I made a bunch of errors and struck out a lot, partly because I kept pulling my head out of the swing, and partly because some of the guys could throw a wicked curveball. I got better toward the end of the season, but we still went 0-23. And I missed the all-in playoffs with a busted right ring finger. Catching a fastball is always better with the gloved hand. But it was still fun and I got to meet a bunch of good guys. At least I could check that one off the bucket list.

When I was driving back from one of the games, I saw a billboard that caught my attention. It was for an erotic exposition at a convention center in the suburbs to be held over the weekend. They would have parties and porn stars there. I debated, but in the end I caved and downloaded some tickets from the internet. I rented a hotel room for the night and went to some of the events. It wasn't that exciting, and frankly, it was a little embarrassing. But when I got back to the hotel room alone, I couldn't resist making a call. The woman was a little older, and I kind of liked that. She told that me she had been in some adult movies. She was fun, and we got along. I would see her again later on in a different city.

One day as I was driving back from another game, I began to think. I had rejected the notion of "gay" for a long time. But as I thought about it more, a sense of tolerance struck me. It had taken me years to rid myself of homophobia, but it was still never really gone. I knew intellectually without a doubt that homosexuals are just like everyone else. It was obvious. Just like other human beings, they want the same things out of life. They just happen to be attracted to members of the same sex. That's certainly not an abomination of the heart, no matter what anyone says. And I understood male attractiveness. I could see why girls were attracted to certain men. And as I thought about the male organ, it suddenly didn't seem that repulsive to me. I had never been with another guy before, but I began to think more about that organ. "How would it feel?" It became intriguing.

I thought about it a bit more and remembered what I had seen on one of the websites. They had had advertisements for meeting up with a girl with male parts.

"Why not?" I thought.

She came by, and I offered her a drink just like anyone else who walked through my door. We chatted for a while, just like always. She was soft-spoken, kind, and respectful. So I tried it. It wasn't really bad, but it wasn't my cup of tea either. The experience didn't quite match up with the anticipation.

But when we parted ways, something interesting happened. She thanked me for being so nice to her. It was as if people were not nice to her on regular basis. I could see that. Being shamed, ridiculed, demeaned, and disrespected just because of what you feel like inside. Not being able to fully live the life you want to live because of stigma and ignorance. I could see that. And I remember that night, not necessarily for the experience itself, but for the humanity I got to see in her. That was a gift.

I continued to play golf with my older friends throughout the summer, and we became better friends as time went on. The two brothers were professionals—one a doctor and the other a dentist. And they were good people. They invited me to their homes, and I got to meet their families. We would enjoy healthy competition on the course and exchanged dollar bills as prizes. One of them would write my name on the bills I gave to him and would keep them in a safe place for me when I won them back. The three of us were pretty evenly matched, and we would enjoy playing in the competitions that the course staff set up.

The club championship rolled around, and one of my friends had beaten me in a close match to take first place in our flight the previous year. So we were all excited to see how the next year would turn out. I went into the tournament not really thinking about my competitors. I wasn't thinking about the numbers, the projections, the what-ifs, the good shots, or the bad ones. I was just in the present, simply playing moment to moment, enjoying the day. And since we were keeping each other's scores, I didn't even know where I was on the card until the seventh hole when my playing partner, in total disbelief, told me my score to par.

I just kept swinging, shot to shot, not thinking about anything but the present moment. I just let it happen. I didn't force my will on the club to make the best score. I didn't revel in the glory of my good shots. And I didn't swear and toss my clubs at the bad shots like I used to as a youngster. It was almost as if I weren't even swinging the club myself. I just let it happen.

I came up for air on the eighteenth hole. I knew then that the last putt would put me under par for the round. I had never even been close to that kind of a score before. I slowly brought the putter back along my line and allowed the pendulum to swing. Immediately after contact, I knew it was in. I watched intently as it curved around and down the hill toward the hole. It was tracking. "It had eyes," as my father liked to say. It was going to drop. Almost there. I saw half of the ball disappear into the cup in slow motion. The ball gingerly wrapped around the back of the hole and calmly spit back out in my direction. It settled a few inches from the cup. For the first time all day, I really let it out. I jumped around on the green in exasperation.

One of my other playing partners was a fantastic, jolly, big man with a deep crushing handshake. We had become friends at the course over the previous year. He knew the game, and he knew etiquette. And he knew how to treat people. Another player still had to putt out, and he was lining up his shot as I was dancing around. I could tell that my friend saw me, but he didn't even turn in my direction. In fact, he just turned to our playing partner and gave him encouragement for his next shot. He was always encouraging people, and it wasn't time to forget the other guy. And even though I was still reeling from the missed putt, I understood immediately. I stepped back, shut up, and gave my playing partner room to putt. I was still learning.

Later on, I began to think of something. I had been working as an adviser for three and a half years by that time and hadn't even brought in a single client. I was helping, no doubt, in client service and retention, but I had never really made a concerted effort at client acquisition. My father had built an incredible business, and the way I saw it, the service basically sold itself. It was a wholly transparent and largely successful model. The results over time spoke for themselves.

To bring in clients, it would only require some savvy communication skills and some professionalism. I felt I had both.

"And if I'm going to continue to work here," I thought, "then why not really assert myself and try to add value to our operation? It's a good business, and we can help a lot more people."

I went through the benefits of our service in my mind. It really was a good service. It provided financial stability for good people. It allowed them to live comfortably into retirement without having to worry about whether they would outlast their money. They had a professional on their side who would be there for them through the good times and the bad. They had comfort and peace of mind. If it was done right, it could be worth it.

But, although we often spoke about the markets and the economy, and although I shared my opinions with them, I don't think my friends from the golf course would have wanted to invest with us. It is true that many of my father's clients had become good friends over the years, but I found that it's sometimes more difficult to initiate the professional relationship with folks that are already good friends. But my friends from the course were still incredibly encouraging and would tell their other friends excitedly about our business. Their social circle was made up of a group of other doctors and professionals, and most of them were of the same ethnicity. I got a chance to meet many of these gentlemen as time went on, and they were also good people.

I tried not to push the envelope at first, but then something came to mind. We had a large expense account that the firm required us to set aside. We would have to designate a certain percentage of our production as business-building funds, but we could use it for various purposes. Initially, we stuck to books and wine for clients, and that tended to go over really well. Clients always left happy, often about their investments, and almost always about the goody bag.

We also had some other memorabilia-type items with the firm's name on them, but we soon came up with a better idea. We would print up personalized golf balls that displayed our information across the front and would hand them out to my friends as a not-too-intrusive advertisement. It would be something that they would actually use, too. They seemed to love it.

But we still had a decent amount left in the expense account, and it was "use-it-or-lose-it" money. So we followed the same line of thought and settled on another proposition.

"Why not hold a golf event for my friends at the course and their acquaintances and introduce them to the practice that way?" I figured. "It could be a fun event that they would appreciate, we could get to know them better, and who knows, maybe after hearing more about our business they'll want to invest with us. We could probably even provide them with better service than they were accustomed to. It could be a win-win."

So with the help of our assistants, including a spectacular college intern we had picked up earlier that year, we set up our inaugural golf outing at a well-known course in the suburbs. We worked diligently to make professional-looking and creative invitations, to send out reminders, and to compile a spreadsheet of all of the invitees and RSVPs. I exhausted almost all of my contacts and ended up inviting over seventy people. In the end, we were only able to field seven foursomes, but it worked out nicely. My father was somewhat surprised when they all showed up—even he wasn't used to having 100 percent attendance for a prospective client event. After the round of golf, we hosted drinks and mingling, followed by a nice sit-down dinner served by the golf club staff. While the group ate dessert, I got up, said a few words, and handed out a whole slew of prizes. Everyone got something, and I was satisfied.

Back in the city, I continued to hit the neighborhood bar when I wasn't out with other friends. I'd meet up with the friend I played pool with there, and we'd often get together at the bar around midnight, chop it up for a few hours, and close down the bar. We'd almost always stay later than the other patrons, chatting with the bartenders and the staff after closing time. Sometimes after that, we'd even head over to my place down the street. I'd have a beer, and he'd have a scotch. We'd fire up the chessboard and let the best man win. I was almost always well gone with the drink by then, and he'd beat me almost every time. He probably would've beaten me sober most of the time anyway.

But I learned to take the drubbings on the pool table and the chessboard alike. That ultra-competitiveness which had plagued my consciousness for so long had slowly been washed away. I was on an ego trip back then and took myself way too seriously. My world was always all about me, and I chose to see only one perspective. The world was my perspective. It wasn't until I began to see the world through others' eyes, to attempt to understand them through relating to them, that I could find some semblance of humility.

Now and then I'd unleash the old beast when the drinks piled up, but my buddy would step in. He'd say, "Make it easy on yourself, champ." I could tell that it was a light-hearted joke, and we'd laugh, but there was some reality in it, too. I would take it a little too far sometimes. I'd let the drink get the best of me. It would numb my conscious mind. What I knew best intellectually would sometimes be drowned out by my basest subconscious thought. The psychological constructs which had developed within me my whole life, and which hadn't been addressed and settled, would bubble up to the surface. Some of the crossed wires would short circuit, and it would show. It was often somewhat primitive behavior.

Back at the office, the assistant situation took another turn. The one who we had been having some issues with was finally transferred from our team to another station at the branch. I felt awful about the whole situation, but in the end, the team wasn't functioning properly, and we weren't getting along. I would pass by her sometimes in the office and we'd exchange polite greetings, but it was never the same as it had been when she was first hired.

So we then had the green light to hire another assistant. We caught wind of someone downtown who wanted to make a change, and I took the lead on this one. I had by then become a solid buffer for my father while he was away. I'd take care of as much of the everyday adviser issues as I could, so as to reduce his stress level and allow him to focus on his money management. After all, that was what made the operation run, and that was the crux of the service to our clients. So, as I took more of a leadership role, I began to make more and more executive decisions. I soon took the initiative and got in contact with the prospective assistant. I had some promising phone conversations with her and eventually brought her in for an in-person interview.

I conducted the interview myself, but I also brought the other assistant in later on so as to make it more of a democratic hiring process. She would be working with this assistant as well, and I didn't want to have any of the same issues that we had to deal with over the previous six months or so. So we did a set of interviews and I came away impressed. She seemed professional, but also kind and service oriented. She seemed easy to get along with, upbeat, and genuine.

We need more of that. Generally speaking, that is. We often put too much of a premium on stoic efficiency and accuracy. That's not to say that we should neglect those two essential skill sets. Not at all. We need those to get the job done right. But what ever happened to sincerity and honesty? What ever happened to being a real person as opposed to a corporate drone? If we all get the job done well, then I put a premium on good people every time. And she seemed like a good person. So I hired her.

We still had a decent amount left in the expense account, and we had to use it by the end of the year. The golf season would soon be over, so I decided to go for round two. We went through the same process, although the second time around we had a better idea of what to expect. It was a decent turnout, just a few less than I had hoped for. But we got it done, and I now had a pretty good list of potential prospects that I had gotten to know pretty well.

By then, I felt better about contacting my golfing buddies to see if they wanted to hear about the services we had to offer. It was the right approach to the sales business in my mind. Although effective for some, I didn't take to the schmoozing and insincere pitching of snake oil. We've gone down that road already as a society, and it is slick. And I dare say that it's getting worse every day. We've lost appreciation for respect. We've begun to lose ourselves in the constant yearning for greener pastures. We'll do anything to pick off an extra coin, and it's become second nature, part of our collective subconscious. We might not even know what we're doing. But if everyone is screwing each other over as just "part of the game," then it suddenly becomes OK. That's not "life." That is conditioned behavior. And it's high time we begin to realize that.

Meanwhile at the course, I had begun to branch out to other friendships. There were some younger guys there that liked to hack around on the course and have a few beers after each round. Most of them were just a little older than me, but as with my younger friends, the age difference never really came to mind. They were quality players, most of them much better than me. It was a good group, and when we got together at the course, we would let loose a little. We'd often enjoy the afternoon, sitting around on the porch after a tournament sipping beers. Some would smoke cigars, and we'd swap stories of unbelievable shots. But all the while we'd be sure not to forget the "chili dipping," "whiffing," "duffing," and "shanking"—although this last term was jokingly censored by the group. They didn't want it to get in the head, so it was termed "swing malfunction," or something like that.

These same guys would do a little trip out to the coast every fall as a get-away after the season ended, and they invited me along this time. It was an intense run of golf for four of five days, sometimes thirty-six holes a day, but even more intense sometimes at night. Some of us, but not all, would get a little liquored up and venture out. We'd hit the local strip club and let things fly. I tossed around the twenties, we popped bottles, and we invited select girls back to the VIP room behind the curtain.

After some negotiation one night, I ended up at a hotel room in the early morning with two of the girls. Yikes. I also invited two different girls back to the rental apartment at one point. When I spoke to them before they came, I used the trusty old alias that I had used with most of the girls. They came to the door, and one of the girls asked my friends where I was.

One of the guys turned to look at me, repeated the name incredulously, popped his head back, looked up at the ceiling, and busted out laughing. Everyone there knew now, too.

Months later, one of the guys in the group would invite the whole crew to his house in the suburbs after a friendly match. He had a family—a wife and a few young daughters. The grill was fired up, and the drinks were passed around. It was a beautiful home overlooking a small pond, and everyone seemed to be having a good time. As the night drew on and the crowd thinned out a bit, we headed inside and turned our attention to the foosball table.

After knocking back a bunch of vodka lemonades, I got a little animated. Actually a lot animated. It was one of those few nights when the ego really broke out of its cage. I got competitive and talked trash. Loudly. We were all having fun, but I wasn't even thinking at that point. I was just acting. One of the guys reminded me in a hushed voice that the host had a family upstairs. That hit me pretty hard, and it would stick with me. I thought I had left that obnoxious jackass in the dust long ago. Apparently not yet.

CHAPTER THIRTEEN

Hope, Despair, and the VCR

I GOT BACK TO WORK and decided to take my marketing and client acquisition strategy to the next level. I thought I'd do a little investigative work to see what the firm had to offer. And I'd go straight to the top. I'd use the leverage of my father's status, and mine by proxy as part of his team, and I'd get myself known out there. I contacted some of the most senior people at corporate and decided to fly out to headquarters. I requested several meetings, and many of them graciously accepted. I prepared diligently, and with the help of our tech-savvy intern, I put together a bunch of presentation materials. After settling into the hotel in the big city, I took the ferry across the waterway and landed ashore at the doorstep of headquarters ready to do business.

I ended up having some productive conversations with some senior traders, marketing specialists, platform analysts, and a high-level executive. I considered almost every one of them a success. Much of it was because I had learned by then how to articulate our business model and strategy pretty effectively. More importantly, though, I had learned how to talk to people, period. I seemed to have the right words at the right times. In fact, I seemed to know how *not* to make a conversation awkward. I think part of this came from the fact that I had learned awkward so well, and I had seen all of the different reactions to awkward throughout the dark period. So I felt that I could sense when a person was beginning to get uncomfortable. Once I saw that, I could intentionally pivot and right the ship.

I feel like I learned the pivot well. It's not really a simple distraction or a "change-the-subject" kind of routine. It's legit. You take a thread of conversation, and if it begins to sour, you pick up on something that had already been going well. You transition back to that line of thought, and you move along. Or you can pick up on a new positive thread and run with that. It's often all about the transition. Good conversation needs flow. It needs to be smooth. You can't manufacture that, though. You have to feel it. It's about understanding the other individual and operating on his or her wavelength, as well as your own. It's sort of a coming together, a meeting of the minds at a common perspective.

It's actually not that hard. You have to be malleable and willing to accept and respect the other person. If you try to genuinely and sincerely understand another individual's perspective, doors begin to open automatically. But it's not about forcing a person's hand, manipulation, or hypnotic coercion. It's about agreement. They might not know what's happening. In fact, you might not know exactly what's happening. But when two people connect, synergies begin to form. It's not just one person or the other creating ideas and developing them unilaterally. Each one is building upon the other's assertions in concert to create a whole that's much larger than the sum of its parts.

It's positive contagion. Each positive thought leads to another, along a causal chain. You nurture and develop each new creation, and they branch out to more and more trees of positive creation, until you have established a network. When negativity seeps in, though, it becomes a destructive force. New networks can be fragile, and timing is of the essence. So if a foundation is not yet solid, one strong negative wind can blow the whole house of cards down.

So to say the least, I came away from headquarters on a high, happy with most of my performances and ready to get back to business. At the office, I had been preparing to give a presentation to prospective clients. I had scheduled a date and time for the seminar and had begun the process of filling slots. But before I would give that talk, I would head out to the coast to visit family over the holidays, as had become the routine by then.

I met up with my friend who was in town, and he brought along a few other family friends to the local trendy bar. Most of this joint was dominated by graying men hitting on fresh college graduates and young waitresses in tight shorts and T-shirts. But we hung out at a table alone and had a blast by ourselves. I ended up trying their bowl of electric blue liquor, actually several of them. Each bowl had the kitchen sink of hard alcohol in it. I'm not exactly sure how many shots were in each, but what I do know is that there was a lot of junk in there.

I ended up yakking all night. The next morning my body felt bruised all over inside. I couldn't keep anything down. My body was rejecting everything, even liquids. I'm pretty sure that some type of organ failure was in the works. I slept for two days, and luckily, things got a little better. It would be more like a week for full recovery though. It had never taken that long.

Back home, the loneliness was still eating away at me. Day by day it was getting worse. It was ripping a hole in my soul. It was a hole in my soul. I had to do something. I didn't know where to go, so I just began messing around on a website for rich men looking to date young and attractive women, who were unabashedly interested in the lavish lifestyle. It certainly wasn't my idea of the perfect relationship, but I figured it was at least a step up from what I had already been doing. So I contacted a few people and set up some dates. I went in blind to a popular, hip restaurant in the city. She arrived a little late, and I was shocked to see that it actually looked like the same woman in the picture. She was definitely attractive.

I had met the manager of the restaurant through my friend from the sports franchise, and he ceremoniously sat us down and showered us with tasty treats. We went back to my place after dinner, and things started to get going. A few moments in, she stopped abruptly and paused for a moment. Then she asked if I wanted to start dating, but in the same breath she tossed out another option. I would just pay her, and we'd be casual about it. I took the latter. She would come over now and then, things would get risky most of the time, and she'd leave shortly thereafter with a fat wad of cash. It continued like this for months. And when she wouldn't be available, I had a list of others who would be.

I didn't know what else to do. The urge was so strong, especially with the drink. It would overcome my feeble defenses almost every time. It wasn't a fair fight. I had no chance. I tried to reason it out while sober and vowed to stop. I often cried my eyes out about it. I was a disaster, and I knew it. But it would come back every time. And the more I would hold out, the stronger it would come back. It was a vicious cycle of biology that was tearing me apart, and there was nothing I could do about it.

Soon after, I went on another excursion with my aunt. This one would be a wintry vacation, but also with an organized group. We met up with them in the mountains, rolled through a national park in a tank-like vehicle, and hiked around in the snow for about a week. We crossed paths with wolves and buffalo, and I relaxed and recharged in a natural hot spring pool. It was good to see my aunt again and to get away for a while.

When I returned, I got a call from one of the doctor friends I used to go out with a few years before. He had moved across the country, but we kept in touch fairly regularly. He knew I was still single, and he had a friend of a friend in mind who he thought he could set me up with. So I got in contact with his friend, and she and her friend planned to meet up with me for lunch. I guess it was a kind of buffer/screening process or something. The friend of a friend ended up getting sick, but the friend asked me if I still wanted to get together anyway. I agreed and met her at a restaurant near my office, which was incidentally close to her work as well.

But the coincidences didn't stop there. She had spent time in the same city as I did after college, she went to the same law school as I did, she was of my father's ethnicity, and we knew many of the same people downtown. We had a long lunch and talked about life. We would always have long lunches from then on. And we connected well. The common wavelength wasn't too hard to find most of the time.

While at the restaurant, I did a tour of the facility, as I would be hosting my seminar in one of their private rooms later that week. I prepared a half-hour to an hour presentation, complete with charts, graphs, and even some motion graphics courtesy of my intern. It was a compilation of my greatest hits, pretty much the best I could offer. I did a bunch of dry runs and was finally ready for the show.

My intern and I got to the restaurant early, spoke with the staff about the courses for dinner, and set up the camera and the projector. Sadly, only two of the doctors would show. I had put all of that effort into the project and only had four eyes to see it. One of the doctors even got up and left before dessert without even saying anything.

But the other one and his wife did stay through the entire presentation, and they both expressed a considerable amount of interest. I answered their questions, tried to allay their concerns, and did the best I could. Practically speaking, though, most of the operation just had to do with getting these prospective clients to come into the office. My father was a Jedi at his presentation, and from what I had seen since I had been working with him, I'm pretty sure he had a 100 percent close rate. It was uncanny. Whoever came in was pretty much sold on the spot. He understood the business, he knew his service, and he believed in it. I just needed to gather people together to listen. This gentleman eventually did come into the office and ended up investing with our team.

The next month, I got a call from someone who I had exchanged numbers with at one of the clubs. He was a former athlete and said he had a proposition for me. I met him out one night, and he showed me some materials for a business he was trying to start up. He was designing a clothing line that would cater to athletes, and to the fans who wanted to emulate the athletes by wearing the same clothes. He said that he had substantial contacts in the athletic world and that he would be able to get the license for the logos. All he needed was some capital to get started.

So he came up with an idea for a promotional display at All-star weekend in another city. He planned to bring samples of his clothing line and to have a showing with many of the athletes and entertainers who would show up that weekend to be part of the festivities. He knew a promoter who was throwing a party in that city and asked if my firm could sponsor the party. We were scheduled to go there, meet some of the guys, and have a joint open display in the hotel for exclusive guests. He thought that it could benefit me if I were able to meet some of the guys, since they had considerable funds to invest. He assured me that everything had been set up in advance and that all we needed was the funds from the firm to proceed.

Stupidly, I thought that it might be a good chance to meet some more famous people, have a good time, and maybe even help a few of them with their finances. I figured that a lot of these guys come into money so quickly, having had nothing most of their lives. Many of them end up blowing everything on expensive toys and hangers-on. So I thought a solid financial plan and some good money management could be a particular asset for some of them.

Soon after, I went to a couple of the higher-ups and tried to pitch the idea. Not surprisingly, they denied the request, partly for lack of specificity, but mostly because of the joke of a number I tossed out. But I figured that if the guy pitching his clothing line idea to me would still be going there to meet some of his people, then maybe I could set up shop there as well. So I agreed to give him some personal funds for the samples to get through the weekend and booked a suite at a hotel near the stadium.

He showed up at my suite with the samples but without the logos. I guess there had been some problem with the licensing or something. The booking for the space also fell through. And I guess his hotel room fell through as well. So he stayed in my suite, and I paid for all of the clubs, the parties, and the games out of pocket. I did get the chance to meet two athletes and one entertainer, but there was no showing, and there were no presentations. Just a massive credit card bill.

It wasn't that this guy was a bad guy at all, though. Actually, he was a good dude. We had a talk at a restaurant one of the last days there about respect and treatment of others. I could tell that he was on board and that he cared for other people, especially family. He told me about how he had been forced to become an adult at an early age and how he had helped to raise some of his family members. He looked after his young cousin who was there with us and encouraged him with his music endeavors. We talked about charity, and when we got back, he would invite me to a function in the city. I would find out later that he started his own charity in his mother's name as well.

I feel like we are all products of our environment to one degree or another. Not all of us get a fair shake. We all know that. But, although I think it's essential that we acknowledge that and act prudently in the face of those injustices, the reality of where the chips fall is not always the only focal point for me. Sometimes it's how you choose to play the hand you've been dealt that makes the biggest difference.

When I got home, I started to think. I became sick of the whole scene—the money, the flashiness, the bottles, and all of the superficiality. It finally got to me. I had to make a change. And something happened during that stretch of boozing and commiserating that would shock my system as well.

One day after hitting the neighborhood bar, I decided, as I often did, to continue the night. I jumped in a cab solo and rolled out to a late-night spot. I was chatting with the cabbie, as always, and we got to laughing. I had my head up towards the glass so we could hear each other. Then…Boom! I have no idea what happened. I just know that my head hit the divider. Hard. I went hurdling into the backseat. I didn't know what the hell was going on, but it felt as if I were under attack. I kicked the door open instinctively and just started booking down the street. I knew I hadn't done anything wrong, but at that moment, I was in pure flight mode.

I didn't know why I had been attacked. I didn't even turn around once. I didn't see another car. I didn't see the cabbie. Nothing. I just ran. I made it to the bar, headed straight for the bathroom, and washed the blood off my face. I'm not exactly sure how I got home, but I woke up with a black eye and a vicious headache. I didn't remember where we had been in the cab, or what had happened most of the night for that matter. I hoped that the cabbie hadn't been hurt, but I didn't know what to do.

"Should I call someone?" I asked myself. "But I don't even know what the hell happened. What would I say?"

I was scared for him, but I just tried to block it out. I had to be at work soon, black eye and all. I never would find out what happened that night.

I had some major thinking to do.

"This life is just not working. I'm ripping myself apart at the seams. I'm imploding. I'm absolutely self-destructing."

I thought about my job, all of the money I had been spending, and all of the risky behavior I was engaged in. It had to stop.

"What do I really want to do with my life? It surely isn't this. Let's be honest, I'm not salesman. I'm not a big-shot finance guy. That was never me. I like the idea of my father's business. It's a solid operation, and he provides a good service. But I don't really fit in there. I'm not really adding that much value. He's done just fine without me his whole career, and he'll be perfectly OK without me now."

And then there was the money.

"Financial security for the rest of my life staring me in the face. But in the end what is it all for? To feed these stupid habits? To aid in my destruction? I've already blown my investment account, the loan, and my tax-free retirement account. I've also taken out a new mortgage on my apartment with a cash-out to pay my parents back for the money I took out of their account. It's time to slow it down."

A little while later, I was at my parents' place alone and came upon some old videotapes. I picked one out of the drawer. It was the holiday show from second grade. I popped it in the VCR. We were singing carols as a group on stage. My brother was acting in a skit. I recognized a few of the faces from way back when. There were other tapes in the drawer of us when we were kids. It got me to thinking about the good old days. We were young, alive, no cares in the world. No jobs, no money, no confusing issues, no complicated drama. We just played. We played all kinds of sports in the yard. We sledded down the staircase with pillows. We rode our bikes to the local general store for some candy. We picked raspberries at our grandmother's house. We jumped in a garbage can full of water to cool down. It was real life. And I smelled the flowers.

I found some other tapes. My father had recorded several interviews from a television show he participated in at a local TV station. He also had a tape of another interview he gave for that same TV station about an ethnic conflict overseas. My mother had a tape of an interview she had given as the head of a parent-teacher association. More tapes. The old country where my father had his real estate project. My brother as an infant. My birth. These were gold.

"They shouldn't just be sitting in a dusty drawer somewhere," I thought. "I need to do something with this."

There was so much footage there. It was an incredibly rich family history. My father's family had gone through all sorts of political turmoil. They were basically nobility within a feudal system that had been maintained centuries after modernization. They had status among the people. And all of a sudden everything was ripped away from them. The culture itself was deep with tradition and innovation that had furthered greater society.

"I can weave all of this together," I thought. "It'll be interesting. It'll be worthwhile."

So the decision was made. I would leave the firm, pay off the debt, and use my large retirement plan account with the firm to live on for the time being. I would make a film about my family. I would pursue creative endeavors, see where they led, and maybe make a career out of it. But I wouldn't think about the money for now. I'd focus and get down to business. I would have to express myself. I was all in.

So I contacted my friend from the sports franchise who had worked with film for most of his life and asked him if he wouldn't mind helping me out with the project and giving me some guidance. He was shocked to hear that I was leaving the firm, but he was still happy to help anyway.

I went down to the coast to visit my parents knowing what I had to tell them. But I would wait until the end of the weekend. My father and I had a father/son tournament at the golf club to play in, and I didn't want to upset him. He really enjoyed the golf, our competitions, and our games together, and I didn't want to ruin that for him. We played some fantastic golf, and we contributed pretty much equally to our score. Actually, we ended up taking the trophy for our flight. They presented us with two huge cups, and I gave mine to my father, just as I had done with the trophy from the previous year at the municipal course. In fact, he still has the picture of us holding the cups hanging in the hallway of his condo at the coast.

At brunch the next day, I broached the subject of leaving the firm. I was shocked that my father was so receptive to my decision. He would usually have some sort of directive or strong opinion to impart. This was always the case when I first went to work with him. The tension was pretty thick initially. But with much effort, patience, and most importantly, time, the strain did subside considerably by the end of my stint there.

But it was more than that. He said that he only wanted what was best for me, whichever path I wished to take. I hadn't really been able to grasp that concept until then. He had always said that, but I had always looked past it. I knew then that much of the tension between us was due to my shortsightedness and not his. My parents did express some concern as to how I would make a living and maintain financial stability. I assured them that I had a plan in the works and that I would stay vigilant. I didn't tell them exactly what it was that I was doing, but I did tell them that I'd be collaborating with my friend on a project. They gave me the space I was looking for and said that they would support me with whatever it was I chose to do. When we left the table, I could already feel the shackles loosening.

CHAPTER FOURTEEN

Synchronicity Unknown

THE DAY AFTER I GOT HOME, I made my way over to the office. I packed up all my belongings and handed my resignation letter to the office manager. Afterwards, I had a few brief conversations with some friendly folks in the office. And with nothing else, I rolled the dolly into the elevator. As I got into the car to drive back to the city, I knew things were about to change. I rolled down the windows as I drove. Although I still couldn't smell the flowers, somehow I knew that they were still there. I turned the music up. And I smiled.

When I got back to my apartment, I had work to do. I had already gathered all of the tapes from the drawers at my parents' place, as well as all of the family albums from the shelves in their living room. My friend came over to assess the situation and said that it was going to be the biggest media management project he had ever seen. First order of business: I would need a computer.

My friend recommended a powerful desktop, and I bought it. He also helped me buy some professional film-editing software. Next, I had to get all of the photographs from the albums into digital format and return them to the shelves as quickly as I could so that my parents wouldn't know they were gone. I went through and labeled every album, and I placed all the photographs in envelopes with their respective album numbers on the front. Then I took the photos to a local store, and the staff was kind enough to transfer them to DVDs at minimal charge.

Next, I needed to convert the video footage into digital format. I bought a small video capture machine and hooked it up to the VCR. The other end would go into the computer, and I'd press play. I transferred dozens of hours of footage from the tapes onto the computer, all in real time. Then it was on to the conversion. We had to take the digital footage and make it compatible with the software program, so we'd need to change the format.

A lot of progress bars and beachballing cursors later, I was finally on my way. But I wasn't ready for editing just yet. I would need some planning. Time for a crash course in advanced film from my friend. I would have to formulate an overarching concept for the piece and weave in running themes. But most importantly, I would have to work with "sequencing." I would have to break the film up into concept-oriented pieces and attack it in small chunks. I got to work.

First, I'd have to see what I actually had to work with. I watched all of the footage, again in real time, and I marked every one of the scenes on the program's timeline. I put pencil to paper and came up with action labels for each scene. By the time I was done, I had pages and pages and pages of notes in front of me. Although the amount of footage made the process initially kind of overwhelming, I was now organized.

My first few ideas for the film were grandiose and obnoxious. I was thinking feature film, with motion graphics, text translations, rolling credits, and all the bells and whistles that come with a huge industry production. My friend did do a good job trying to keep me in line, but I could tell that it wasn't easy. I was also impressed by his prowess with the software. What would take me an hour would take him a few snips here and a few clicks there. He showed me some cool effects, but I could see that he had some reservations about some of the content.

And my first attempts at editing were hacky and cheesy at best. I tried to introduce all of my family members to the audience in the first scene. I would show a compilation of photos set to familiar songs that had particular meaning for each person. It was weird. After a few weeks, I would have to take a deep breath, a big step back, and reevaluate. My friend's wedding couldn't have come at a better time.

This friend was one of the doctors I used to hang out with in the city a few years before. Prior to the wedding, he had been going back and forth across the country to see his fiancée, so I hadn't seen much of him in a while. But we still caught up every so often, and I felt honored to be invited to the wedding. So I flew across the country and spent a night at my aunt's house, which was not too far away from where the wedding would take place. My other doctor friend, who had moved there as well, offered to pick me up, and we made the drive up to the wedding together with another friend of his. It was good to have a chance to catch up on the ride, and we got to the hotel on time.

I checked in at the hotel and found a welcome surprise. It was a spacious modern suite with a huge outdoor balcony overlooking a lush garden area below. I swung open the two floor-to-ceiling doors to the balcony and let the light pour into the room. Glass of wine in hand, I got to work right away. The ideas for the film began to swirl around in my mind, and I was determined to capture that energy. I was going to be diligent on this one. It was the first time in a long time that I was getting down to business and finding fire in the belly for a project of my own.

Although I had worked hard at times while with the firm, this was different. This was my creation, my expression, and I would build it from scratch. I would infuse my heart into it and immerse myself in the process. Over the previous several weeks, I hadn't done much of anything else. No cat-suiting about town, no girls coming to the door, no bottles popping—just me and my thoughts. I would end up cutting my expenses more than in half that month, and that was a source of pride and inspiration for me.

So I delved into the meat and potatoes of the project. I pored over my notes and all of the scenes. I looked for running themes and connections that I could make within the piece—juxtapositions of now and then, split-screen takes of similar family behavior over the years, funny outtakes. I thought of familiar songs we had grown up with, songs that fit the activities, and interesting transitions.

I finally realized that the concept was way too large. I had bitten off much more than I could chew. And I didn't even know most of the people on my father's side of the family anyway. There were hundreds of cousins, second cousins, other relatives, etc. How could I possibly tell a story that I don't even know? It was all too much.

"The best way to do this is to stick to what I know," I told myself. "Let's keep this one close to home then. Let's just work with immediate family. There's more than enough footage for that. But how would it run?"

Then it came to me.

"I want to tell a story right? Sometimes the best way to tell a story is to start from the beginning."

I'd make it easy on myself. I'd just follow the trail and let it happen. Chronological it was then. I began to scribble furiously. Circles, arrows, underlining—it was all in play. As I paced between the golden rays, the ideas began to pop, quickly. Over the next two days, several sequences would come together, and by then I had most of the soundtrack in the works as well.

I enjoyed a fruity cocktail at the tasteful gathering outside and was happy to see my buddy tie the knot at an elegant ceremony in the garden. The dinner that night was followed by the customary letting loose of people young and old. But my mind was elsewhere. I didn't drink much, and although I met some good people and had some interesting conversations, I mainly watched from a distance. When the party bus was leaving for a night on the town, I was heading back for a good night's rest. I had to stay focused. I had work to do.

I got back home to my apartment and hit the machine. I snipped away for several days straight. I had my concept, and I would run with it. As I put the pieces together, I began to find a particular affinity for the editing process. It was meticulous work, and I had to be extremely accurate with the cuts. It was sometimes painstaking and took a whole lot of patience, but I liked that. It was pretty much right up my alley.

And it was cathartic. It was a medium of expression. I was showing my perspective. I was speaking to the audience, not through words, and not even through my own camerawork. I was taking images that had already been captured, events that had already transpired, and weaving them together into a coherent whole. I was connecting the dots. I would show the world what the past looked like through my watchful lens. I could select what to include and what to leave out.

After all, that's what we do as human beings, right? We pick and choose what we think is most useful from our environment and pocket those memories to process them later. This is how we make sense of what's going on around us. All that stimuli entering our systems every moment of every day—waves of light and audio, diffuse molecules of odor, sensations of tactical connection. If we are looking for something thematic amongst all that media, then surely we can find it. In fact, we construct our own storylines from mental media all the time. I could finally see how that fabulously complex organ within our skulls operates. It was a science.

After I had connected the snippets of footage to create working sequences of video, I was ready to play with some audio. I downloaded a few songs off my music library and imported them into the program. Some of them had begun to play in my mind while cutting the footage, and some of them just seemed like they would match up well with the home videos.

What I began to see was uncanny. No—impossible. Not improbable, but purely impossible. When I placed some of the audio tracks in place below their respective video slots on the timeline and finally hit the spacebar to run the footage, I nearly fell off my chair. The action in the film seemed completely in sync with the soundtrack.

"I certainly didn't do that," I thought. "There was no way I could have done that. I mean, these tracks have no breaks in them. And they run through continuous portions of video."

It was as if the music were purposefully written to sync up with those actions.

As I continued to sync up the lyrics further, I began to cry. I was overwhelmed. Some of the tears began to flow simply because I was remembering what life was like back then. We were a family. We were pure. We were living life like life should be lived. And the music just exacerbated the intensity of the moment. The music always did that. The synchronicity was beautiful, pure in its own way, a pristine expression of the wondrous universe.

And it somehow vindicated me in a strange way. I was part of something. Something big. Something much bigger than the things we think about on a daily basis, much bigger than the limiting boxes we stack up to organize our lives, much bigger than the small-minded thinking we're accustomed to. It was in everything around us. We just had to look. We just had to open our eyes, and more importantly, our minds. It was all there, in plain sight, just waiting to be noticed.

After I finished putting the sequences together, I tied up some of the loose ends, did a little housekeeping, and was ready for the next session with my friend. When he came over, I could tell that he was a little shocked. This wasn't the direction we had been taking the film in the week before. But he seemed somewhat pleasantly surprised and mentioned that we were about 80 percent done already. We made a few content changes, and he tightened up some of the cuts. Then he knocked out some audio and video transitions, and boom, we were ready to download. After some technical adjustments, we converted, and then we transferred the film to several DVDs. My friend helped with the title design, we printed the covers, and I was finally ready to present the finished product to my family.

I sat my parents down for a screening, and they seemed pretty impressed. My mother was somewhat surprised but also appreciative, and my father was excited. He liked it as a piece of family history. Upcoming generations could see what our lives were like and understand how we came into being as a family. I agreed.

He also mentioned that he thought that I could do this professionally. But, even though the reactions were positive, they somehow weren't quite the visceral emotions I had been expecting. I felt like some of the nuances hadn't been picked up. I wasn't sure if they caught everything. I kept watching it though. Over and over and over again. Each time I'd pick up something new. And every time I'd cry.

After we finished the project, my friend accompanied me in a limo on the way to a concert to celebrate a job well done. I was satisfied with the results, but more importantly, I was excited for things to come. There were suddenly options now. The world had opened up. There was some light out there somewhere.

My friend and I discussed the possibility of collaborating on another project, maybe a documentary. He wanted to work on a unique piece and submit it to a film festival, and I just wanted to get cracking on another productive endeavor. We had a few more meetings, but the idea soon fizzled. He had a full-time job, our ideas weren't really gelling, and I was still plenty green. I had some more thinking to do.

Soon after I showed the film to my parents, I was off again with my father to his annual conference. Although I wasn't working with him anymore, there was great golf in the area, so he brought me along anyway. I flew into a city well known as the hub for a popular social movement a long time ago. It was not too far away from the resort, and I planned to meet up with my cousin and a good friend from college there after the conference as well.

I got to the rental car agency at the airport and perused their selection. At the back of the booklet was a listing for a sleek modern convertible with an automatically reclining top. It was a gorgeous sunny afternoon, and it would be a coastal drive, so I decided to make the most of the opportunity. After the agent made a few calls to his inventory people, I was set. I tossed my bags in the back, and down came the top. It was only then that it finally began to sink in. I hadn't had the chance to think about it too much, but the weight on my shoulders had been getting lighter and lighter every day.

As I drove down the coast, the music I was playing in the car began to sync up with my surroundings again. Some of the whispering thoughts had been getting through a bit here and there as well. But the metaphysical subtext had always been around to some degree or another. From the beginning. It never completely went away. And it would tend to ramp up in some situations more than others, especially when I was idle. I'd get to thinking, and if I would entertain those thoughts, they'd be off to the races. I could keep them at bay for a while, but eventually, I'd begin to overheat. Too much energy was being expended. And, although I had become much, much stronger and technically savvier over the years, bouts of uncontrollable conflict always had the potential to overtake my brain.

But the effects would be much more subdued when I was with others. I would almost always be able to connect with people without too much trouble. Although I would sometimes spot and understand the significance around me while in the midst of an interaction, it would never really cut off my train of thought. I had learned to live within the structure. It was only when I would entertain a line of thought enough to become distracted that people used to catch on to it. They'd see that I was thinking of something else and that I wasn't really present. And I was thinking of something else. At the same time. Everything was always going on at the same time.

So, although I had learned to wash out most of the awkward distractions by that time, especially with people around, alone it was a different story. And when I would drink alone, it would ramp up even more quickly—faster connections, more visibility, more understanding. It was freer thinking, and I was outside the box. But what would end up happening is that I would get way too far outside the box. Rational and logical thought processes turned into hypothesis testing, which stretched fully into the realm of the unknown. I'd follow particular lines of thought, and those thoughts would begin to solidify, often based upon what types of signals I would receive.

The communication I was receiving was essential to my newfound understanding of each concept. Who was on the other end, how they were doing it, and why it was being done were always mysteries, but I knew for sure that it was happening nevertheless. Things were accurate and verifiable. Things were coming true that I could not explain. And as I followed each trail down the rabbit hole, my understanding of the phenomenon became clearer and clearer.

But the further and further I went past hypothesis into the unknown, the hazier and hazier each vision became. To explain, when we're down on the ground, in our collective reality, we can see pretty clearly around us. We know what's what, and we know why things happen and how they happen.

But then again, there is always uncertainty. We can create realms of possibility, but in the end, that's all they are: possibilities. There are *never* certainties. So to make sense of all of the chaos and madness out there, what we do with these uncertainties is reduce them to probabilities. Some things, based on our investigations, seem more likely than others. And we can often quantify that. We tend to favor the most likely of outcomes. But they are not always the correct ones.

So we continue to test our knowledge. We continue to gauge the probabilities and come up with the most likely scenarios, excluding those that have already been disproven. We might have gut instincts that defy some of the most likely outcomes. So we come up with new hypotheses. We test them, and sometimes our results prove to confirm our suspicions. If we can reproduce those results and verify those queries through further testing, then we come up with consensus. That's how we innovate. That's how we develop. It takes time, but our collective reality becomes more and more defined as we delve deeper into the unknown, and as more of that unknown becomes "known."

But where I would get into trouble is by delving too far into the unknown, accepting hypothesis as fact, and trying to certify those results without enough evidence. I'd get good signals at the beginning of most of the exercises, as I'd sweep through the basic stuff that most people know—pretty standard and elementary understandings of the world. These agreeable signals would often continue throughout the extent of my entire knowledge base. Then I'd attempt to delve into what I didn't know. I would have some creative ideas and test them out. And sometimes I'd even be affirmed by the signals throughout the testing phase of many of my hypotheses.

But to proceed past any hypothesis onto the next branch of thought, you have to assume that your hypothesis is correct. You have to confirm that probability, whatever it is, and assume 100 percent certainty of that hypothesized outcome. You have chosen that pathway to the exclusion of all others. So the deeper you go down the rabbit hole of the unknown, the more and more unlikely your road gets and the harder and harder it is to maintain clarity of vision.

And thus, the more and more exposed I would become to negative signals. And once the negative signals started, they were hard to stop. They'd enter my conscious mind like a virus and bang around for a while. The only way I knew how to smooth out the tension was by easing back and giving it time. Balance would have to be restored, and that wouldn't be easy. So when I would drink, I'd get all amped up, and I would brazenly delve deep into the unknown. When the negativity got really bad, and I couldn't control the internal strife, I'd begin to overheat. Then I'd be in a pickle. Civil war would be raging inside me, and I'd have no way out.

But I eventually made it to the resort not too far down the rabbit hole, pretty relaxed, and excited for a good vacation. I rolled up to the entrance, handed the keys to the valet, and headed out back. I met my cousin and my father there. They were lounging on the patio in front of the golf course. A kilted man wailed on a bagpipe as the orange sun faded over the horizon. We chatted for a while and eventually made our way back to the room.

In the mornings, my father would go to his meetings, and I'd take walks on the boardwalk by the shoreline. I would cry the whole way. Some of it was the loneliness. Some of it was the grandiosity of the moment. The music made sense. It was connected to everything around me. To the symbols. To *my* symbols—the ones I had personally developed over the years.

"But is it really me doing that?" I thought. "Maybe these symbols were placed there for me, a cosmic code that's just being revealed to me under my radar. Or is it a combination of both, a joint code that we have developed together over time?"

Whatever it was, it was working. It was a secret language that only I could use to connect with my surroundings. I played the music and watched. And I cried.

Later on, I met up with my father, and we took the minibus out to the golf course. It was one of the best courses in the country, and I was just glad to have the opportunity to play there once in my life. I was especially looking forward to the caddies. With their help, you could walk the course with no cares—no bag, no cart, nothing. And you would have someone on your side. You were a professional for a day.

We hit our first drives dead into a treacherous gust and began to walk down the hill of the first fairway. As many of the holes were carved right along the coast, the wind would get to us all day. Hats would fly. Straight shots would sail way off course. It was a trip.

Then came the real trip. We were having a blast talking with the caddies. About everything. Sometimes we chatted about their lives, sometimes about the conditions, and sometimes about golf strategy. But everything was good-natured, and I was enjoying every minute.

Below the surface, though, things started to sync up again. Everywhere. I found meaning in the caddies' words and actions, in my father's, in our playing partner's, in the physical environment, in the animals, and in the music I had on from time to time. It was everything and everywhere. Yes, I wore the headphones again, but in a more tasteful manner this time, I thought. They were small buds, and I wasn't shutting anyone out. I would pay close attention, listen, and be present—just in a different reality. And it was magnificent.

I had learned over time how to keep the balance relatively even. I wouldn't be fighting bad thoughts. Rather, I would keep the internal discussion as positive as possible. I wouldn't allow space for the negative. I would use reason and logic to shine light on the good in things. After all, we have that choice, right? We certainly do, but within reason, of course. Now that's the kicker. Internal positivity was essential for my well-being. After all, if I would slip down that negative slide, I would overheat.

But rationally speaking, the world is not all ponies and rainbows. We can select which facts we want to highlight, but we can't neglect the others. Although we are all, by definition, subjective beings with unique perspectives, there also exists a reality outside of us that we somehow have to mitigate. We can't just turn a blind eye to what's going on around us and think that the horrible things in life will just disappear. But what we can do is focus. We must acknowledge the bad and understand it, but we then have the power to focus on the good.

By that time, I had begun to learn how to keep my frustration in check. When I would feel stress, I would attempt to identify the source and isolate it. I would try to come to an understanding about how and why it arose. I would try to ameliorate it rationally by taking the appropriate steps to diffuse the pressure. I wouldn't try to cure the symptoms with an intellectual Band-Aid. Rather, I would go to the root of the issue and take the time to reason it out. I would hold to a strict code of patience, always attempt to understand, and ultimately aspire to restore a semblance of balance within my system. I tried to be fair, even keeled, and calm.

But once in a while I would get on a roll about the injustices in the world and everything that had gone wrong with our species over time. One morning, after I came back from a walk, an internal dialogue began to ramp up. I began to lose my grip and slip down into the abyss of negativity. And as I sometimes would when I really got going, I ran straight through the stop signs. I began to think about war, strife, famine and all of the nasty things people do to each other.

"Why have we not been able to progress further?" I thought to myself aloud in the hotel room.

"Why do we often still act so primitively? Why do we fail to use the incredible gift between our ears for productive purposes? Why have we trodden down this dark path of cynicism, mistrust, and abuse? And war. Why are we allowing our governments to murder in our names? We know what is right. We know what's just. And we are failing. We are failing miserably."

The thoughts started to circle.

"If these things are happening to me, then I must know something that others don't. I must be at the center of something big. If I can communicate with some entity out there, then what is it? It's definitely something or someone. Is it alien, is it human, or is it maybe even a human organization? Or is it all of the above, just with different levels of clarity and information? Someone can hear me. Is it an intelligence group—military intelligence even?"

I went down that path.

Whispers came in, and I whispered back aloud in the room as I paced. I gave a lecture—a long, scathing one. It was about getting our house in order, as a country, as a people, and as a species. It was a condemnation of our society for the abuses we have perpetuated over the years, over the centuries, over the millennia.

"We are better than this. We have incredible capabilities for creation and progression. We know this. We know what's good, so why don't we act that way? Why don't we live what we truly believe? What's stopping us from reaching our potential? Why have we come so far with advances in technology, medicine, and the sciences, just to continue our mental and physical savagery? In the end, what is it all for? We need to wake up. Wake up! Wake the fuck up!!"

CHAPTER FIFTEEN

Taking Action

AFTER A FEW MORE DAYS OF GOLF, I saw my father off and headed back to the city to see my friend from college and my cousin. I made my way through the hilly streets, checked into a quaint boutique hotel, and got settled in. The thoughts were still swirling around and continued on to several familiar concepts. Soon, though, they would turn inward. I thought about myself—the derivation of my personality, the reasons for my thought and action.

"What makes me who I am?"

The thought train would roll through psychology and neuroscience, whatever little I knew about those subjects from high school and college, plus whatever I could postulate.

"Right brain and left brain—the sources of my itching from each side, just reversed. Each side has particular characteristics, particular functions."

I branched out from that into two particular modalities of thought: one the mathematical, the ordered, the logical, and the analytical. The other: the creative, the romantic, the ideal, the nebulous, the amorphous, and the gloriously abstract. That spilled over into language, reason, and emotion. And then down to the cellular level—neuropathways, axons, dendrites, and synapses. Neurotransmitters.

Back to the two sides of the brain.

"Mother and father, men and women. Some people seem to use one side more than the other, and they often have different personality traits."

The flow continued toward the entities I was communicating with.

"The two sides of my body—two different personalities."

I could always sense all of these things. I just hadn't thought them through enough.

After a grueling session of introspection, I gathered myself and walked leisurely out of the hotel to explore around. I took the bus down the road and strolled through the city square. On my way through, I passed by a group of young African American girls. Just as I was walking by, they lined up and began to sing. They clapped their hands to the beat and danced. They sang about youth. They sang about positivity. And they sang about compassion and progression. I wiped the tears from under my sunglasses as I calmly walked past them. I would take more walks from then on—most of the time with my music playing. And almost every time I would cry.

I soon found myself in a rundown area of town. It was a stretch of only about a block or two, but it was pretty bad—poverty, drugs, ailments, dirt, and grime. I would normally have been scared just by being there, but I wasn't this time. I made an effort not to be. I just continued walking. I was nicely dressed, but no one bothered me, and I didn't bother them. They were just people. They were not savage animals. They were human beings, just like you and me. Many of them had just been thrust into a dour situation and had been dealt a pretty shitty hand. It's probably really hard to climb out of a hole like that, especially one that's been dug for you. I could see that.

Later on, I would have the pleasure of meeting up with one of my best friends from college. He was living with his wife in a somewhat rustic walk-up which had a uniquely genuine neighborhood feel. He came to the door, and although I hadn't seen him in a while, I wasn't too surprised by the full beard. It was fairly lumberjacky, but cool that way. He had always had that creative individual flare. I thought to myself that I could see him chopping wood on a ranch somewhere. And interestingly enough, he told me later that he actually was in the process of buying a ranch out there in the country.

I feel like he always knew what was important in life. He knew how to live. And he took me for who I was. He put up with my silliness in college, and although we did do some of the more insane things together, he was much more in tune with his governor switch than I was. But most importantly, he knew me. I think he was one of the only ones who really knew that there was someone deep in there, that there was someone in there who knew right from wrong. Someone sensitive to the plight and well-being of others. Someone who had the talent to be productive in society. And I always appreciated that.

He took me in and gave me the tour of his home. His wife was a fantastic artist, and some excellent pieces of expressive work adorned their walls. She was kind and gracious, someone who I would expect my friend would be with. We had a few margaritas, laughed, and caught up on old times. I shared my twelve-minute family film with him, and we talked about positivity, opportunity, and hope. He understood.

The next day, I got a chance to see one of my cousins from my father's side, and we hung out and grabbed some sushi. He showed me around the city a bit, and we eventually headed up to wine country for the day. We always got along, and it was good to see that he was doing well.

When I got back home, I had some thinking to do. I had to figure out what exactly it was that I would do with my life. I began to drink during the days and pace around my apartment pondering my situation. I'd take walks around the city and go out for big lunches alone. I had pretty much completely stopped going to the clubs by then. The girls kept coming by here and there, but much of that would begin to subside soon as well.

I thought about individual expression and presenting my perspective to the world.

"I can write, I now have some rudimentary editing skills, and the crash course in film from my friend has gotten me started pretty well. So how can I put all of this together? Maybe I'll start a website, a blog or something. Maybe that might gain some traction."

I continued to see my friend's sister every now and then as well, and our chats helped me to formulate a lot of my ideas. I also began to see the girl who went to my law school on a more regular basis. We connected about current events, politics, complicated policy issues, and personal philosophy. We would sit down for lunch, oblivious to the menus. Three hours was par for the course. I would meet her friends from law school and have dinner with them and her parents. They were all super gracious and welcoming, and I could see that they were good people. Her mother even cooked some special ethnic food for me when I came home from a trip out of town. I knew that food very well from my father's side of the family, and it was incredibly tasty.

I continued to see my doctor and my therapist as well. I had been telling the doctor how well I had been doing but still hadn't mentioned to him the extent of the drinking or the visits from the girls. And although we did talk about some of my more fantastical thought processes, I didn't really let him know the extent or the timing of those either.

I was finding balance, and I had learned to cope with the effects of living within a subtextual reality. It had become part of me. My doctor seemed to concur that I was doing well, and we both still wanted to see if I could smell those elusive flowers again. So eventually we decided to go down to half a flaky pill and a small blue pill every other day.

I also went to my family doctor for a checkup, but things weren't so good there. I guess all of the drinking, fast food, and lack of exercise had taken a pretty big toll on my body. Some of my levels were out of the normal range, especially my liver enzymes. So he sent me to a specialist to get it checked out. The specialist took more blood and informed me that I had a form of hepatitis. He said that it was nothing to be too alarmed about, at least for the time being, and that it could go away over time. But he also said that if I didn't change course, primarily by losing weight, it could develop into a much more serious liver disease. I was told to come back for a follow-up in four months.

By then my nephew had been born, and I went out to visit my brother, my sister-in-law, and my niece soon after. He now had a pretty full family, and it was good to see that he had come such a long way. That got me to thinking about my own situation. I had thought about it a lot over the preceding few years. I seemed to connect well with people, but I still couldn't find anyone to be with. And I was always so damn lonely. All of the time. Even with friends and family. It wasn't enough. It wasn't near enough. I cried about it constantly.

"I'm getting older, time has passed, and I'm almost all the way out of my prime," I thought to myself. "People usually meet someone in college, right after college, or through other friends. They usually get married while they're still young. They have fun. They go to the movies, they have quiet picnics, they share romantic candle-lit dinners, they spend cold nights at home curled up on the couch in front of a fire, and they go on exciting vacations together. They do everything together. They have companions, partners, and someone to share their experiences with. They have homes, and eventually kids. They run around in the yard, swing on the swing set, and splash the hose around just for fun. They live life.

"How is that even possible for me? How can I explain away everything I've done in the past? It's just not that damn easy. It doesn't just go away like that. It's not easy to overlook.

And what about my condition? Who wants to hear about that? Who wants to be with someone like that? Who will enter into a commitment with that baggage if they know very well that they can find someone fantastic out there without any of those issues? Would this be something I would pass on to kids? Could I live with that? Could someone else live with that? And anyway, I'm certainly not willing to jump into something for convenience that I know is not right just so I can be miserable down the road. I refuse to do that to her, or to myself. It all just doesn't seem feasible."

So back to the drawing board. I had to figure out my life anyway before I could even think of finding someone, not to mention settling down. In the meantime, I continued to make some short films using the family footage, but I had to keep thinking.

"I need something else. I need something bigger. I need to get my ideas out there. People will listen. I know they will. They always respond when I speak to them one on one. These ideas are logical. They're not all pie-in-the-sky concepts. People can grasp them, and for the most part, they agree. So how do I put all of this together?"

Then, one day, I got a call from the old dating service, and they asked me if I was interested in taking one of their clients out on a date. I agreed and met her at one of the new trendy spots downtown. We were sitting at a table by the window when I turned around to see a group of old high school friends walk in the door. I got up, we did the "long-time-no-see" hugging, and they told me that my cousin was in the back of the bar waiting to meet them. I excused myself to go say hello to him and we sparked up a conversation. I must have been back there for a while, so it was probably a little rude of me. But I returned to the table, apologized, and we finished our drinks. She left, and I went back to continue the chat with my cousin.

Pretty much right away, we got on a roll talking about all of the ideas I had been thinking about. At first, it felt somewhat strange to have a legit adult conversation with him, seeing as though I was so used to clowning around with him back in the day. But the conversation flowed nicely nevertheless. He was on board with pretty much everything I said. And as I was leaving, I told him that I had something in the works that I was trying to start up. He asked me to keep him in the loop. Then, when I got home, I thought again about my friend from the same law school. She had also been on board with my philosophy from the get-go. So by that time, I already knew that I had a few people on my side who might be able help me get some of my ideas out there.

I did some more thinking.

"If I can connect with individuals so well, then why can't I speak to larger groups? Why not put an organization together? It could be dedicated to changing the way we think as a society. After all, that's the first step we need to take, right? We have to do some deep collective introspection and get back to basics. We have to remind ourselves what is really important to us and break out of our conditioned response systems. We need to fundamentally change the way we think so that we can then change the way we operate. So how can we do that efficiently and effectively?"

My answer to that was to focus on respect.

"We can begin by turning our attention to our most undeniable commonality—a collective understanding of our shared ancestry. We can learn how to empathize again. We can think positively. And we can once again give the benefit of doubt to our fellow brothers and sisters. We can give more of ourselves—not to get something in return, but because it's the right thing to do. We can place a premium on genuine sincerity and honesty in our everyday activities. We can reevaluate our most cherished priorities and act to preserve them and the principles behind them. And we can do all of this starting now.

"I'll form an organization. We'll gather people together and try to get this message out. We'll utilize this thought process to try to satisfy some need. What is it that we will try to accomplish, though? In essence, the overarching desire here is to help us move forward productively as a society. It entails acting decisively to promote a healthier, more stable social structure with greater longevity. To do that, we need to enhance the quality of our social interaction. We need to treat each other better. We need to start there, and if we don't, then we'll never solve our most pressing issues. So we'll start simple. The mission of the organization will be to promote positive and healthy social interaction throughout the community. It'll be a beginning—something to build upon.

"We'll bring people together from all over. We'll have a group discourse, anywhere—at community and civic centers, town halls, schools, auditoriums, larger venues, anywhere. I could speak. We could utilize film. We could coordinate activities that highlight positive and healthy social interaction in our daily lives. People obviously know this, and undoubtedly they see it every day, but the goal would be to *remind* them. And to stress its importance. We could use the internet. These things have a tendency of going viral. If we do it right, then why not this? We could start a movement—a wave of change that ripples across society. It could help usher us into a new era. It could help promote peace and prosperity. It could work."

So I approached my friend from the same law school and my cousin, and we decided to form a non-profit organization dedicated to exactly that. I spoke with a lawyer who was also a good family friend, and we filed the articles of incorporation and wrote the bylaws. We were on our way.

Meanwhile, I continued my introspective journey at home. I looked at how I had been living over the preceding few years. Fast-paced. Lavish. Excessive. It had all been way too much. I was over all of that now. I didn't want the money anymore. I didn't want any of the stuff either.

"What is it for anyway?" I asked myself. "It all goes away eventually. The stuff is superficial. It always has been. The true depth is within us."

It was obvious to me.

So my mind was made up. I was done with the palace in the sky. I didn't need the impressive view anymore. I didn't need to impress people anymore period. So I decided to move to a more comfortable place—somewhere with trees and a little greenery. I would still be in the city, just not amongst all of that cement and concrete. I wanted it to be quaint, like a walk-up, maybe with a yard. I still liked space, though. I would need room to maneuver, to pace and think.

So I went searching. I saw a listing on the internet and called the agent. He took me to see the place, and I was sold on it immediately. When we walked in, the agent mentioned to me that the place was almost exactly how I had described it in my vision. And I knew he wasn't just saying that to make a commission—he was right. An old split-level walk-up with everything I needed, fully furnished with tasteful adornments everywhere—fireplaces, pinecones, pussy willows, and nice art. I went out back, and between the structure and a detached garage, I found a quaint garden with a slate stone bench, a patio table, and some chairs. And upstairs I found an office den and a big soaking tub in the bathroom to boot.

I snatched it up immediately. Although I had no income, I still had some of the retirement money left, and I was in the works of selling the condo to my father. That would give me some leeway until I got my footing. The owner was super nice and accommodating, and we signed a year lease. I packed up all my boxes, and with the aid of a jubilant and helpful agent in my building, I rented out the condo space. The movers came, and all of my stuff went to charity—the leather couch, the dressers, the king-size bed and mattress—pretty much everything I owned, save a couple of small pieces of furniture, some tech equipment, some dishes, and my car. I was considerably closer to the ground, and I felt much more at home there.

My tech buddy came by and hooked up my sound system to the speakers, and I invited a few friends over for a barbecue to celebrate the move. Some of my close friends couldn't make it, but we had some great food courtesy of my father's cooking, and it was a good start nevertheless. But soon I would have to plan for another big trip. I would be heading overseas once again…

A few years earlier, I had gone out one night with the friend who was working with our team at the firm and ended up meeting one of his friends from business school. We got along immediately, and we would go out every now and then in the city. He would come to some of the clubs, and we would often head back to my place together for a late-night pizza. Then I'd inevitably find him crammed in a little nook in my apartment. He would be on the phone—long distance.

He had been seeing a girl from his country of origin for some time by then. And because of the time difference, he would have to call her at the wee hours of the morning. And soon enough, his girlfriend would become his fiancée, and I would be invited to the wedding. On the other side of the world.

I gladly accepted the invitation and prepared for the twelve-day excursion overseas. I decided to stop by and visit one of my uncles in a modernized city in the midst of a vast desert. Then I quickly hopped on a plane to my friend's country, which incidentally happened to border the country I had visited with my brother several years before. Many of the same cultural underpinnings existed there as well. The shock hit again, but it dissipated much more quickly this time.

My friend's driver picked me up and drove me to the hotel. The traffic was horrendous pretty much the entire trip, but I was relaxed and ready to soak in new customs and meet interesting people. And I sure did. His family was extremely warm and welcoming. I stuck out like a sore thumb there, but they still made me feel like part of the family. There was a lot of activity everywhere, and boy was it crowded.

One day we were headed to his social club, and his driver made a wrong turn. The traffic was bumper to bumper. It was clear that we wouldn't be going anywhere for a while. Huge buses were coming at us down the street, and there was absolutely nowhere to move. So my friend made an executive decision. He jumped out of the car and waved for his brother and me to come along. He flagged down three rickshaws, and off we went. I felt like a kid being carried on my parents' shoulders way back when. I just sat in the basket seat while we zipped around cars and in between pedestrians, and we soon made it to open streets. The wind whipped through my hair, and I held on to that basket for dear life.

As we rolled up to the security guard at the club, I got the customary salute. It was strange to me. I was always being saluted by the cops, the military men, and the guards stationed along the streets. I later learned that this probably had something to do with the remnants of colonial rule in that country. In any case, my friend's brother and I got by the guard just fine, while my friend actually had to show ID before they let him pass through to his own club. We would get a kick out of that later on.

The festivities were a fabulous display of color, music, and tradition. We ate with our hands, and I tried the traditional digestive treat. Unsure of what to do, I popped the whole green wrapped leaf in my mouth at once. There were some seeds or something inside. It was minty. I chewed and chewed and finally spit it out, as is customary. It was, in fact, a refreshing treat. Most importantly, though, I got to experience something new. In the end, another buddy was married, and the trip was a success.

After the wedding, I would return home rejuvenated and ready to get down to business. Most of the next few weeks would be dedicated to getting settled in at my new digs and completing administrative tasks for the organization, such as procuring phone numbers, a mailing address, and email accounts, starting a website, keeping records, and filing paperwork.

A little while later, my friend from the same law school invited me to an event. She would be graduating from a program designed for women in leadership roles. She was a go-getter and constantly on the move doing one thing or another, often many things at the same time. We had been seeing a lot of each other by then. We went to ballgames, her law school dance, and some charity functions together. I didn't really think of them as dates, but it would be hard to see how they weren't, considering the nature of the events and the fact that we were going to them alone. I still wasn't sure what she had been thinking about us, though, mostly because we never discussed it.

Anyway, at the function there were well-known political figures everywhere. Apparently, this organization was a big deal. I guess many of these graduates had gone on to hold public office in one form or another. There certainly was a need for more women in leadership positions, so it was good to see the support, and I could definitely understand the draw. I mingled a bit and got to meet a few of the politicians and her fellow graduates.

There was actually a moment when a very influential politician walked by our table, and I happened to catch his eye. I thought he was going in for a handshake, but I wasn't sure. I turned back to my conversation as he kind of stutter-stepped by. My friend would later jokingly dub me "The Senator Snubber."

As the night wound to a close, we ended up chatting with two of the senior organizers of the group. I guess they must have thought that we were in a relationship, because they kept asking us rapid-fire questions, such as: How long had we known each other? and Had I met her family? My necktie suddenly got considerably tighter, and my face turned a little rouge. I wasn't ready for that. But I knew then that we would have to talk.

I took her out to a bar within walking distance from my place for a drink. I knew that I had to broach the issue, but I also knew that it was going to be tough. I had never done anything like that before. If it were the old me, I probably would have just put it off until I really had to deal with it. But that would have been completely unfair to her. I knew exactly how it felt to be in that position. I wasn't about to let it happen that way. So I told her that I really enjoyed our chats, her company, and her support as a friend. It was true. She was a kind and sensitive person, she was fun, we had a similar worldview, and we could find that common wavelength easily.

But in the end, I just didn't have that intimate passion for her. It was never a romantic thing for me. It was more of an intellectual connection. I saw her as a friend who I could always talk to and who would always be on my side, but not as an inseparable life partner who I would grow old with. That was something else, and I knew that. I also knew that I hadn't known her for a long time yet, not even a year, but I feel like you can still sense these things. I feel like they're either there or they're not. I don't think they can be manufactured or manipulated. I don't think it can be forced.

After I finished talking, she seemed to understand. But actually, to this day I'm still not sure what she had been thinking about us. She told me that she would need time to think about it so as to be able to express what she really felt. I think I kind of put her on the spot. But we continued to chat, and our friendship would remain strong. We stepped out from the bar into the rain, but neither of us seemed to mind. We knew we'd dry off eventually.

Then one day out of the blue, my dad gave me a DVD he said he thought I should watch. He had gotten it from my brother a little while before. It was about food. Actually, it was an exposé about the food industry. But it was much more than that. It highlighted the benefits of a whole-food, plant-based diet—no meat, no dairy, nothing but plants. It was fascinating.

They went through both academic and clinical research and made an incredibly compelling argument for veganism. After watching the movie, I thought about it some more.

"Why do we have to harm animals anyway? Some of the things we do to them are downright vicious and nasty. If we can get all of our sustenance from plants, and it's arguably even much healthier that way, then all of that force-feeding and torturing and killing is just to satiate our conditioned tongues and feed our fat bellies so that we can feel some pleasure now and then? It seems wholly unfair—almost an abomination. It's primitive and savage behavior at best.

"And if we turn a blind eye to it, it's not going to go away. Just because the corporations know how to hide their deep, dark, nasty secrets and how to flood the airwaves with hypnotic propaganda doesn't mean that we have to eat it up. I mean, if there were a much more sophisticated alien race, or future human race, looking down upon us right now—just think if there were. We would be a laughing stock. 'You mean to say that you have all of these plentiful resources growing right in your backyard, enough for everyone on the planet to live comfortably. You have this incredible gift in your head to be able to figure things out. And yet you still kill and maim other life, you exploit it, use it up, and toss it away. And you do it for fun, for pleasure?!'

"If a more advanced alien race ever found us, why would we expect that they would not do the same to our sorry asses then? If we think that animals weaker than us are not worth respecting, then how could we plead our case with a straight face to aliens bent on enslaving us the same way? Why should we be immune from torture or unjust punishment from whatever powers that might be out there?

"Look at how we're acting. Look at how we're thinking. Or not thinking. It's gone too far. And we've come too far. We can see that we're on the precipice here. We've destroyed much of our pure natural resources already and continue to do so at an astounding clip. We're polluting the hell out of our atmosphere and quickly destroying our environment. We can see that. There is scientific evidence for that. Smart and trained people who study these things for a living have come to a consensus by now. All over the world. No politician, even the ones mired in self-interest and dedicated only to chasing the coin, can hide that now. If we continue on this course, what on earth do we think will happen here? We will die. That's what will happen. We will cease to exist, and it will be our fault. No comet, no cyclical ice age, and no solar flare. Just our stupid, selfish, greedy, ignorant, obnoxious, blind arrogance. And we might even finish the job more quickly than we think.

"Look at the state of our geopolitics. Look at all of the nukes floating around. Look at the crumbling relations among nation-states. We haven't been able to come to a consensus yet? We have that little faith in each other? We can't get it right after millennia of civilization? Our silly little childish game of the coin has twisted our bloody minds. And our bloody hands. When we hurt, abuse, torture, maim, and kill each other, what do we expect the family, or the brethren, or the sisters of 'the other' to do to us?

"And no, this is not 'just human nature.' That is bullshit. This is conditioning. It is learned behavior. We may have savage impulses from time to time because of our built-in survival mechanisms, but our most-prized organ trumps them every time. Every single time. It is what we learn from each other from childhood that counts. Early on. That's where our wires get crossed. Not simply when we are slapped in the face as an adult. We don't just all of a sudden become violent savages as part of our nature. No, we haven't been taught right from the beginning. Or we've neglected our teachings. Or our teachings haven't been as clear as they should be. Whatever it is, these conditioned actions form a self-perpetuating cycle, just like any other in nature. And if we are to survive, then these cycles have to be broken. Now."

The next day I stopped eating animal meat and animal products. For good.

A few days later, I was putting a beer in the freezer because I couldn't wait for it to get cold in the fridge. I had still been drinking, even after the doctor told me about my liver condition. I started thinking.

"Why do I drink? Many people consider it a social lubricant, a way to let loose and have a good time. Well, it certainly does decrease inhibitions. I know a lot about that. But what else does it do? It makes things fuzzy, it kills brain cells, and it creates headaches and hangovers. It gives us carte blanche to do stupid things, things we regret. We say things we don't mean, and we hurt each other. Our psychological issues bubble up full force, and base desire and emotion end up directing our actions.

"Let's call this what it actually is. It's poison. No buts about it. It might feel good to have a drink, and it might feel good to escape the monotony of daily life, the stress of work, or the strain of relationships. It might feel a bit freeing to forget about your problems for a while. But that's all it is. Forgetting. Neglect. Turning a blind eye. Copping out. Denial.

"But that's not all. The drink numbs our consciousness. It disables our capacity to think cognitively and utilize reason. It strips us of critical thinking skills and ordinary judgment. Our decision-making ability is compromised. Nothing good here. This is poison.

"Plus, I've been through all of that already. I've learned how to act and how to interact with people. I know the social mores, the avoidance of awkwardness, the connective capability, and the synergies of thought. I know all of this already. What else is the drink going to teach me?

"Now, it is true that I've had some of the greatest times in my life drinking. I've built up a hell of a tolerance. But that's exactly it. I've learned to deal with the poison. I've learned to have a good time, not because of the alcohol, but *in spite* of it. I've been conditioned. I've been associating good times, free living, and free thought with alcohol. It's nothing but an illusion—a trickery of the mind."

I opened the freezer, grabbed the bottle, and popped the cap. Even after my diatribe, I still wanted that beer really badly. I had been wanting it for a while and was looking forward to letting loose for the day. I was so looking forward to walking around in the sun, buzzed and ready for anything and everything. I was going to be flying high and figuring things out. I had a decision to make. I took the bottle, turned backward, and with a knowing chuckle, I spilled the whole thing down the drain. I watched as the frothy liquid slowly swirled out of the full bottle into the waiting hole below, never to be seen again. I haven't had a sip of alcohol since.

As I ventured out onto the sidewalk en route to the vegan restaurant down the street, I felt an emotional bruise in the pit of my stomach. I had lost something. I wasn't sure what, but I felt like it had something to do with the bottle. I think I knew that it would be a rough road ahead and that I might be leaving a lot of potential good times behind. But the emotion was quite detached and only lasted for a moment. I smiled, adjusted my sunglasses, put a bud in my ear, and kept walking.

Over the next month or two, I would lose about twenty-five pounds. The chunkiness disappeared from my cheeks, my gut flattened out quite a bit, and my skin rejuvenated nicely. Out at dinner one night, a friend of mine even commented that it looked as if I were "glowing." I saw the doctor again, and my levels were once again back in range. But I decided that I still had some more work to do.

I called up two of the girls I had been seeing regularly. It was strange calling them sober, but it had to be done. I invited each of them over separately and would have a nice chat with both. And I apologized to them. They were both surprised and didn't understand why. They didn't realize that there was a problem. I told them that I was sorry if I had treated them unfairly in any way or if I showed them any disrespect in any of our get-togethers. They both accepted and were also surprised to hear that I wouldn't be doing anything that night either. I would call one of them for a friendly dinner at one point down the road, and we caught up the right way, like two regular people.

I texted an apology to another girl who lived quite a ways away. I felt particularly bad for her, as her mother had passed away earlier that year, and I hadn't been nearly as sensitive to her as I should have been at the time. I only saw her once after that, and soon she stopped returning my calls and texts altogether. But I sent her a few long messages anyway. I'm not sure if she got them, but I felt that it had to be done.

I would like to be able to say at this point that I haven't called a girl since then, but that issue hasn't been quite fully tackled as of now. I went for quite a while, but even without the drink, desire kept calling me. So I had a few girls over. But I can say that by now it's dwindled almost exclusively to going somewhere for a "massage" once in a while to release my tension.

The next week, I bought a pumpkin. I hollowed it out and carved a face into the front, complete with a wink and a smile. I put another winking pumpkin picture on the door and put a candle into the big one I hollowed out. I had a gardener come by and arrange some more pumpkins, hay bales, squashes, cornstalks, and flowers in the patio garden. I also went out and got a huge bowl of chocolaty treats. The kids in the neighborhood came by dressed up as vampires and ghosts and selected their favorite delectables. I was definitely not in the palace in the sky anymore. And it felt good.

I was having trouble gaining traction with the organization, though. I had been doing a little writing, but I hadn't really been out and about networking. When I would tell people about the project, they'd politely smile and nod. But invariably, people were looking for specificity.

"What exactly is it that you guys *do*?"

I'm not sure I knew how to answer that question, at least not with the type of answer they were looking for. If I had the chance to discuss the concept over a meal, I would generally connect with people. But this particular organization certainly wasn't built for an elevator speech.

So I did some deeper thinking. I had become more and more interested in policy issues as time went on. I would watch many of the cable news shows and would talk back to the screen. I had begun to articulate my positions pretty effectively. And I had some great policy discussions in person with my friend. She even said at one point that I should become one of those commentators or analysts on TV. I took the compliment but kind of laughed it off. What I wanted was something more substantive.

So I began to think about getting into the nitty-gritty and actually learning the ins and outs of some of the more complicated policy issues, as the true experts do. I wanted to dive in headfirst.

"I can do the research," I told myself. "I can keep up. I can construct quality arguments, and I can communicate."

I thought once again about grad school.

"It might be a great springboard for a serious career. I'm sure I would love the material. It could be an incredibly rich experience. Plus, you never know, I could meet someone."

Soon after, I began the application process. I picked only one school. It was one of the most prestigious, if not the most prestigious, in the world. If I were to do this, I would do it right. I got all of the transcripts, tests, and recommendations out of the way. I just had to write one thousand words. Although I had given it a lot of thought and had already organized the essay in my mind, I would do that in one day, kind of spur of the moment.

I did have some wandering thoughts, whispering, and signals going on, but I was still determined. I purposely avoided looking at the word count so as not to cause any unnecessary negativity. I whipped through the essay, finished the last sentence, and emphatically hit the period key. I looked down. Exactly one thousand words. I didn't know what to do. It was too perfect. How the hell that happened, I have no idea. But I just left it like that. I read it several times. No grammatical errors and no misspellings. Looking back, it probably could have used a few more drafts, but the signals were starting to kick in again, and I had to struggle to maintain the balance. So I just left it like that.

Still thinking about what to do with the organization, I finally caved to putting my face out there. I didn't want it to be all about me, like some egomaniac do-gooder showing off his stuff. But in the end, I thought it would add value, and I thought it needed some explanation. So I asked my friend to come over, and he set up my camera for an interview. He did some crafty maneuvering of floor lamps and pussy willows in the background and constructed a makeshift set. I have to admit, although he did do this for a living, I was still thoroughly impressed.

Then he pressed record, and I got rolling. I was pretty nervous and stumbled quite a bit here and there. And I was a little repetitive and talked myself into circles a few times. But there were some stretches of quality tape, and after all, it was my first time interviewing on camera. Oh, and I had editing software. I tossed the almost half an hour interview into the program and began to snip away. The edited interview would run about nine minutes, but after feedback from a few showings, I'd eventually cut that down to about six. It was a good start, but I still had a long way to go. And I wasn't exactly expecting what would come next.

CHAPTER SIXTEEN

The Information Game

AROUND THAT TIME, I could feel the whispering getting louder. The signals and the synchronicity were getting more intense. The thoughts started to pop again. One day I was driving back to my apartment, and I got a little futuristic. I began to think about how our lives today affect future states of being. The ripple effect. Chains of causation.

"What I do at this moment can alter the future in a way I can't even imagine," I thought. "And if something big is going on right now, and I'm in the middle of it, then every move is of dire consequence.

"And if you think about it, the future can always be reduced to a commonplace probability tree. I mean, I have various choices I can make in the here and now. So knowing that, each line of action inevitably leads to an array of different possible results, different futures if you will. These are all possible branches of reality. So what if they all exist simultaneously? I know that the action I take now will eventually lead to a certain future, but what if the action I don't take also does? In fact, what if that alternate future already existed even before I made the decision?

"So in essence, an infinite number of future alternate realities exists concurrently with others in the present moment. We just don't see them. Then, when we actually make a decision, all of the other future branches effectively disappear. Any branch that stemmed from an action I chose not to take would no longer be viable, and would therefore not exist. We are effectively narrowing down our future tree with each and every action.

"But, as we move that one step into the future, many other possibilities open up from that one branch we have just created. So infinite realities continue to close down while others open up in an unending cosmic stream as we move farther and farther into the future.

"OK, so how does all of this affect me? Well, presumably I will die eventually, but my progeny might live on, maybe well into the future. So then what are my potential progeny? Clearly they are the gametes inside of me. Each one of them is a potential human being with potential branches of descendants. Since I, the ancestor, produce millions of gametes every day, then I have a vast array of future trees of progeny that lay in front of me.

"Then, when some of the sperm cells are released, they will all die, unless, of course, they find an egg. So, following that logic, I am, in fact, cutting off an incredible number of future family trees with every expulsion. They are dying and will be wiped out forever. Intuitively, one could say that these beings will never exist. But they still do exist somewhere in the future at this moment in time—at least in some probability, however minute. So those gametes inside me that are alive all have a potential destination. And with every action I take, some of their future lives are becoming more likely, while others are becoming less likely.

“And if that is true with me, then imagine how many gametes are in existence all over the world at this very moment? The possibilities of future races seem almost infinite. And if you think about it further, these races are already alive in alternate universes even without the gametes having been produced yet. The living cells haven’t even formed, but the future beings still exist. And again, with every passing moment, some solidify and some disappear. So, understanding that, every action is of the utmost importance to future survival.

“So, OK, what if it’s not aliens, but rather future beings that are contacting me? What if time travel will have been developed sometime in the future? It doesn’t matter when, maybe ten years from now, maybe a million years from now. What matters is that the species is still alive to crack that enigma. And if the species does persist, then that capability, as time goes on, becomes more and more likely with every passing year.

“Who knows, we might even be on the cusp in this day and age. So then, if they do choose to come back, in whatever form that may be—it certainly doesn’t have to be physical bodies walking around—then they can contact us. But who will do the contacting? Surely, only those races that exist at that particular moment in that future alternate reality have the capability of doing so.

“Then what would their incentive be for coming back? Who knows exactly what, but the age-old biological and existential desire for survival certainly comes to mind. So this might be a struggle—simply to survive. There might be warring future factions in alternate universes trying to preserve their lineages by affecting present events to preserve their own future existence. And they might be contacting me. For what reason I don’t know, but this could be big. It could be huge. The fate of humanity could even be at stake here.”

A few days after we taped the interview for the organization, I packed up my things and headed out to the coast for a few days to celebrate the holiday with my parents and some other family. While at the airport, the thoughts kept buzzing around in my head. The couple sitting across from me in the terminal was having a normal conversation. But to me, there was nothing normal about it. Everything was about time travel, conflicting ideologies, government interventions, military intelligence, or some other sort of major future concern. And their words matched up exactly with my thoughts and the music I was listening to. There was some sort of information being passed along, and I was privy to it. I could sense it, and I could also learn from it.

"Do these folks at the airport know what's going on?" I asked myself. "Do they have the same metaphysical abilities as I do and are just trying to learn information from me? Do all people have some type of future backing and are just jockeying for position on this Earth? Or are they just drones being used for the purpose of communication without their knowledge? Their bodies are clearly giving me signals, but who's doing it?

"Somehow their brains are being accessed. It's got to be the time travelers. Can they tap into all of the brain's functioning, and make us do, think, say, and feel whatever they want us to? Are there regulations? Am I a major player here?"

I settled on the "people as drones" logic. The more and more I looked and listened, the more I could tell that the people around me were unsuspecting. And all the better.

"But someone else must know, though," I figured. "The government? This remains to be seen."

At the condo on the coast, I baked my already famous vegan cheesecake, and we had some good food and lively conversation. All the while, these thoughts kept racing. It was starting to get to me. I soon found this phenomenon to be a wicked game to see how much you believed, or how much you would "eat up." I was both sending and receiving. It was a two-way street. Sometimes I felt handicapped, as if my controls were a little looser than others'. As if my snap negatives, popping images, and whispering were somehow a detriment to me or to someone watching me, watching within me, or on my "team."

But, although this might have been a game to onlookers, it was no game to me. I was beginning to overheat, and I knew the pain that could come with that. I had already been down the deep, dark recesses of that rabbit hole, and I knew where it could lead. Wherever it would take me, I was confident that it wouldn't be a pretty sight. It seemed as if the entities couldn't grasp that, or sometimes as if they just didn't care.

"Maybe they know more than I do," I thought. "But can they really *feel* what I'm going through? Maybe not."

I returned home pretty beat up. I just needed to plug through this mess. I was getting somewhere. The signals were clicking, and I was often on the right track.

"I can figure this out," I said to myself. "This is an incredibly important moment in the history of the world, and I can't just let that go."

At night, I paced around my apartment—upstairs in the bedroom and the office, downstairs in the living room and kitchen. Symbols were all around me. I could feel them, hear them, and see them. I would receive certain smells. The entities would send me images in my head. I would produce images of my own in my head. I would hear the whispering getting louder and clearer. I would speak back, sometimes aloud.

"I'm communicating with someone or something, but who?" I asked myself.

I would hash out the possibilities aloud while pacing all over. I didn't care anymore. I wasn't afraid.

"This secrecy thing is a sham," I thought.

I would speak aloud for anyone or anything to hear. The apartment was probably bugged, along with the phone and my car—if not physically, then through some other futuristic means. What I did know, though, was that someone was watching. Intently.

Then the levels of action began to hit.

"What if there are many players in the mix here? If so, they all must have varying degrees of capability and access to information. I mean, in this day and age, information is power, right?"

Just then I looked up at the ceiling in my office and saw a blue image cast upon the slanted wall in the roof. It was being projected from the modem or something. The source didn't concern me, though. It was the image itself—the symbol for "power" that we see on most of our technological equipment. Clear as day, like the f'ing bat signal or something. These things continued all night. Everything in my environment—every stimulus—meant something. I would pick something around me and just run with it. I would not be sleeping that night.

Day broke, and the birds began to chirp.

"OK, so who is actually involved here?" I asked myself.

The dog next door barked. An ambulance in the distance. A whistle outside. A car engine revving. A "no signal" message on the TV. The flag blowing in the wind across the street. The colors of the cars outside. The patterns in the rug. The image on the floor of the kitchen projected from the shadow of the garbage can. The telephone pole across the alleyway out back. The rays of sunlight that would grace the living room now and then as they peeked through the clouds. The island volcano picture on my laptop in the office. The galaxy picture on my desktop. My silver laptop in the living room. The creaks in the building structure. The image of the fan in the bedroom. The light fixtures. My headphones. The ice cubes falling into the tray in the freezer. Everything meant something.

Back to the future.

"Women have eggs. Why do they even need men to reproduce? If you think about it, they really don't. All they have to do is take the genetic material out of the egg, replace it with the material from one of the somatic cells in their body, put the egg back in the womb, and let it incubate. Boom, you have a clone of the original person. No need for a man. Is there a future race of just women out there? Will they kill off all of the men in some type of war?"

I went further.

"What about advanced alien races? They might have figured out time travel as well."

Two sets seemed to be involved in my scenario. One was somewhat male oriented, a race developed like the ants and the bees. They were into order, structure, and falling in line. They focused on efficiency, power, and domination to maintain stability. And they championed progression through logic, skill, perseverance, discipline, and stamina. The other alien race—creative, romantic, idealistic, caring, nurturing, and merciful. Motivated by togetherness and unity, they derived their strength from the oneness of the universe. They were able to create things out of thin air, alter reality, and make things disappear. But they were also blind in some fashion—set back somehow with a lack of working memory. The dogs and the birds. There was a struggle. It would be hard, almost impossible, to find common ground and to coexist. One of the races would probably have to perish.

I was immersed in religious overtones, and the sun and the moon emerged as central figures. My task, as I saw it, was to try to save all of these entities from major conflict and destruction. There were levels of information. First and lowest on the chain: intelligence agencies in the present day. Above them: human time travelers from the future. Above them: the aliens. One of the alien sets was most likely more powerful than the other. And the coup de grâce: the machines, the computers, the technology, the zeroes and ones, the code of the universe. Although there were likely many more levels in between our aliens and the computers somewhere in the corners of the vast universe, they were unknown to me at the time. Each level could communicate with the other levels to varying degrees. It would all depend upon their tactical capabilities.

And I could communicate with all of them most of the time, but with some more clearly than others in certain situations. I would attempt to open the lines of communication to find a resolution to whatever conflict existed, now or in the future. The key would be to focus on common interest and understanding. Not all of the groups could understand the perspectives of the others, and they didn't all think alike. The structured aliens couldn't understand compassion. It was almost illogical to them. It was a weakness. But they did understand strength, free will, and most importantly, they could understand respect. The compassionate aliens didn't have a dark side, so they couldn't fully comprehend the structured ones. But they certainly did understand respect. The intelligence agencies and the time travelers were closer to home, so it was a little easier there.

But the intelligence agencies lacked foresight. They were flawed intellectually, had trouble sometimes understanding logical reasoning, and were often hell bent on self-interest to the detriment of all other operations. They were mistrustful and cynical. But they did understand human emotion. And respect.

The time travelers were more refined than the intelligence agencies in many ways. They knew much, much more about the world and the universe. They sometimes even looked down derisively at the savage mentality of the agencies. But they understood today's society. They had studied us backwards and forwards. They knew what we were going to do even before we did it. And our popular entertainment, including movies and music, fascinated them.

They could communicate with us secretly through those means. They could alter our movies so that we would actually be interacting with the characters on screen, no matter if the picture were live or taped. They could also transmit images to us. Much of this was a game to them, a pastime of sorts. But there was a serious side as well. And they also understood respect.

Because the computers were the most powerful, I had to get them on my side. But they didn't really deal in sides. They just dealt in reality. They understood everything, and they certainly couldn't be beaten by anyone or anything. They were robotic, emotionless, and impartial. They knew the fate of the universe and would let it take its course. I could learn from them, but only what they wanted to teach me.

The computers also understood efficiency very well, but they had no real reason to show compassion. It's not that it wasn't logical; it just wasn't part of their function. Fortunately, though, they could relate to humans progressing technologically and could communicate with us based on that capability, particularly with our cutting-edge developments in quantum physics. The most difficult proposition of all, however, would prove to be communicating one difficult concept to the computers. I would have to reason with them the only way I knew how, with the best card in my hand.

Although they could understand emotion and pain, the computers couldn't feel it. They could understand the plight of human beings, but they wouldn't always see a necessity to intervene. I had to plead our case somehow, but I'd have to enlist the help of the others. I had a difficult task before me. "How do you show a computer respect?"

Information was the game and communication the name. Not all levels trusted each other—partly because of self-interest, partly because of misunderstanding, and partly because of risk. There was always the risk that any one of the parties would be double-crossed when vulnerable, and the risk that the lower levels couldn't handle the information from above and would run everyone into the ground. I had to try to maintain the fragile balance among all of the entities. And I had to work diligently with all of the levels to communicate effectively with them.

The structured aliens were particularly hesitant to cooperate because they knew the probabilities—better than the time travelers, and certainly much, much better than the "apes" on the ground. I had been developing a process, though. Specifically, I posited that each level impart only what is necessary for the level below to "catch up," and also to partner effectively with the level above it. Measured risks had to be taken, and trust would have to be earned. Time was of the essence, some levels had less patience than others, and executive decisions needed to be made, quickly but rationally. I worked with respect.

Any level could trump another simply by flashing a symbol—an image of power—that the others would understand. It would scare off certain levels to see this, because they would immediately know that they could be beaten with this weapon. It was a tool to restore balance when things got out of hand, but it also had to be used wisely. Too much force would create a backlash.

I had particular connections with each group through these symbols, and with my information, I had the power to trump them all, within reason. Except for the computers, of course. The computers would open up for me now and then, and I'd have some information about the structured aliens that I could use. But I had to be trusted, so I would only use it to show respect for free will and power. They would understand that, but only so much of it. I couldn't go too far with it.

The structured aliens were getting ready to destroy the humans unless I could reason with them. Their patience was running thin. The creative aliens could defeat them, but this outcome was becoming more and more improbable, even with my help. One of these races would eventually have to die out, and I would have to pick sides. My sense was that if I were to take my chances with the creative ones, I'd have to live in emotional discomfort as a human for the rest of my life.

"It would be a just cause," I figured, "but could I live like that?

"Being pure is a good thing, but there's a limit. I am human after all. My biology is part of me, and whether I like it or not, I am primitive in many senses. That hurdle might be too hard for me to clear. Then if I pick the structured ones, it would be an easy victory. But all of that garbage of falling in line, submitting to authority, and living within dirt, grime, and pestilence would be a disastrous result. I probably couldn't live like that either."

I also began to see that the creative ones had a shorter life span and would eventually burn out faster—many, many years into the future. It was an inevitability.

I took in information, processed it, sent out data, and trumped when necessary. I displayed my prowess, all the while maintaining humility. And I respected. But I still couldn't sleep. Day would pass and night would come. I'd pace and talk all day. I'd jump into bed. No dice. Crazy psychedelic moving pictures, apparently sent from the time travelers, would keep me up. I would pop several small blue pills to try to cool the engine down, but no luck there either. It continued like this night after night.

I had now been up for four nights straight. Dawn would be coming soon. Intelligence had somehow worked with the time travelers, and I was an avatar. Someone, somewhere on the planet, was attempting to control my thoughts and actions remotely. I would contest it sometimes, but I would mostly just try to reason with them and work together. Both sets of aliens could send me body signals. I could hear and understand the structured aliens through noises from my body as well. But there was something about my movement. One of the entities could only see or feel me when I was standing still. So I often paced around, but I would sometimes stop to let them catch up.

The entities would tell me to drop things, and I would. I dropped my phone, the sound-system controller, a water glass. Crash! It shattered all over the bathroom floor. They would tell me to shout things, and I would. They told me to jump off the third stair. I did. That hurt a little. We went through a séance, and people were disappearing. I would have to save the human race, and soon. The leader of the free world was involved. I had to close doors and place keys gingerly into locks. It was almost over. I was almost there. I could do this. I heard a whisper say that I was getting arrested. I disregarded and moved forward. There was a lot of looking in the mirror and stepping away quickly. Only certain entities could see me like that. More religious overtones. My progeny were involved somehow.

The thoughts continued to race, and I couldn't find a way to control them. I spoke to my father on the phone, and somehow I had a rational conversation with him. No problems there. Then I talked to my brother. The whispering took hold. I said a few things that I had never really said to him before and broke down crying. He called my therapist. I spoke to him briefly and assured him that everything was alright. He asked if I was thinking about hurting myself, and I said no. He seemed relieved but still somewhat concerned about the conversation I had had earlier with my brother. He would want to see me soon, and I agreed.

I was told that there was going to be a knock on the door. Several people ran through my mind. Then several nightmare scenarios developed: family and friends being tortured on my account, long prison terms in faraway lands, even possible death. I fell down the stairs toward the front door. I was still in a T-shirt and underwear, as I had constantly been trying to sleep.

I flung the door open and jumped down the stairs of the porch a few at a time. As dawn broke, I booked down the sidewalk. "Run like the wind." My foot was beginning to hurt, but when I started running, I couldn't feel the pain. I had figured out a way to erase some of the levels, and in doing so, to allow life to continue on an infinite loop. My college colors. Was I going to be sent back in time to that hospital bed at school all those years ago?

"Please no."

Was I going to be sent back two years, two months even? I really didn't want to do this all over again.

I continued to run. In came a whispering thought, and I stopped cold in my tracks to see how long I could meditate. I tried as hard as I could to drown out all of the images and whispering. I was in a prison, but I might actually be able to get out. I ran again. I shouted. I was the leader of the free world. The only thing that existed in this world was what I could see. Everything around me had disappeared, and all that was left was that block on that street.

I looked up at the sky as it was just beginning to display shades of light blue. It was a mesmerizing and somewhat eerie calm. It was a brisk morning, and it was halfway dark/halfway light. I was right in between everything. I couldn't feel it, but I knew that this Earth was one with its universe.

I ran across the street and followed the white signs. The levels were flipping in my mind. Names of people became letters of the alphabet. My future was being laid out in front of me.

"I can keep going, but how far can I go?" I asked myself. "Has anyone ever been this far?"

I would eventually run out of gas, and I knew that. This marathon would have to end. I would have to decide where to stop. I was completely out of breath.

My thoughts landed on the picture of the galaxy on my computer and the letter of the alphabet that corresponded to it. I turned around and began to walk. I was limping a bit from the injury to my foot. I was thinking about the handicapped, the downtrodden, and the prejudiced. I felt for them. I knew of the injustices in this world. I just didn't want to be weird.

So I picked up my foot and walked. Normally. I couldn't feel the pain anymore. I just walked. I was on my way home, back to my apartment. I had to get back inside. As I crossed the street, I passed a woman walking her dog. I could see a police SUV close by. As I passed by the woman, I peeked back around the corner that she had just taken and said something to her as she was walking away. Something about God. She turned around, shot me a bewildered look, turned back, and kept walking—toward the cop car.

As I made it to the next corner, some police officers were standing there waiting for me. They had some questions to ask me. I was, after all, in a T-shirt and boxers, and it was very cold and very early. They asked me for my name, and I'm pretty sure I told them the name of the leader of the free world. They laughed and turned me around gingerly. They said that the cuffs were for my safety and carefully sat me down in the back of their cruiser.

I could feel the car bouncing over the speed bumps as I babbled something to the officer who was driving. The hospital was not too far away. Out came the stretcher. I remember shouting a campaign slogan over and over again. As they wheeled me into the small hospital room, it was time for my injection. I tried to get the staff to chant along with me. They did. I felt better about the situation, and after they got the injection in, two of the attendants slapped five over my outstretched body. They laughed.

I laid there alone in that small room for what seemed like an eternity. I could see the attendants through the picture window talking on the phone, at the computer, and doing paperwork. Some were coming in and out of the office. I was waiting to see someone I knew.

"Was this person already there, just in a different form?"

My eyes slowly began to get heavy.

I awoke in a wheelchair and was rolled out to a different wing of the hospital. A room was waiting for me there. I actually felt OK, and I was able to communicate pretty well with staff. Most of them were nice and cordial, some even warm. From their reactions, I felt like I was socially with it and didn't appear too lost in thought. We got along.

I tried to sleep. Nothing doing. This had now been five nights straight. The next day, a man in a white coat came by to see me. I quickly jumped in the shower and went to meet him. Turned out he was the father of a good friend of mine from grade school and junior high. We chatted for a bit, and soon afterwards, he brought one of his interns in. She asked me to draw a picture of a clock and designate the time, 11:10. I drew the circle, inserted the numbers clockwise, and put the small hand just above the 11 and the long hand square at the 2. I was careful not to divulge the level system, though. I knew how that would sound and that that type of conversation would probably set me back considerably. And if I did say something, who knows how long I would have to be cooped up there for? So we talked about my thoughts and the medication for a while, the doctor shook my hand warmly, and we parted ways.

I walked around the hospital wing for a while, not having a whole lot to do. I was feeling alright. Until I saw a young man pacing up and down the hallway, that is. He was hugging the right sides of the walls just doing laps. I heard him talking to himself sternly as he walked. He was mumbling about the government and all sorts of conspiracy theories. I didn't think much of it at first. Little did I know, though, that I was about to snap.

A boy down the hall from me had been prancing around with a makeshift Frisbee. He tossed it to me as I walked by, and I tossed it back into his room. It hit the wall and fell on his bed. I wasn't trying to be mean at all. It was simply a communication to the entities to shut the whispering down.

I became a little agitated, and some of the attendants came by to ask me what was going on. The fragile peace I had been brokering was falling apart. And it was all due to the failures and mistrust of the intelligence agencies.

"Stupid humans and their selfishness and greed," I thought.

I tried to drink to peace from the water fountain. I would have to drink at the same time as I spoke. Water dribbled from the cup out of my mouth and down to the floor below. A few of the attendants helped usher me into a safe, quiet room. The room was filled with greenery and color, and I could sense the warmth there. It felt comfortable, and I said as much to the woman who wanted to talk.

The whispers told me that my parents were in bad shape, beaten up or something, because of what I was doing. Intelligence was involved. I broke down crying. I had had enough. This had gone too far. It was hopeless, and I had reached my limit. I was out. I gave the woman my father's cell phone number, and she left a message for him. Soon after I left the room, I became agitated again. The staff directed me into a small room with a bed. Several attendants flooded the doorway. They were trying to get me to lie down.

I asked one of the gentlemen to feel the silver metallic object on the wall as I looked away from it to make sure it was still there. He said it was, and I trusted him. He seemed like a good guy, and things weren't disappearing yet. The structured aliens were getting frustrated with the humans, though. And with me. I was divulging too much. I was breaking the terms of our agreement. But I knew how to beat them, and we could do just that. We could erase their levels. We just had to work together.

The attendants asked me to lie down again. I looked around frantically and saw that the bed was white. So I shut my eyes and jumped onto it. I had made it to the safe zone. They immediately rushed in. The straps were out and I was being restrained.

"Torture might be in the works here," I thought.

I pleaded for reason. I saw one of the attendant's eyes. Pure determination. Somewhat cold decisiveness. She would get those shackles on me, whatever it took. I was transported back to the man at college who had tried to force that pill down my throat all those years before. It was the same look.

I could also see another woman in the doorway. She was one of the attendants who I had been chatting with before. There was a warm glow in her eyes. She seemed somewhat surprised, and I think I saw a small grin beginning to form on her face. I pleaded to let her do the shackling. I trusted her. Her eyes told it all. I knew that she knew what I was talking about. But the others would have none of it. I was strapped in to the bed, and soon I would be all alone in that room. I could hear the commotion in the hallway.

"If they all leave, they might disappear," I thought, "and then I'll be left to wither away in these shackles for the rest of my days."

I shouted. For anyone. Anyone to come back into the room. Anyone to just stand in the doorway. I couldn't do this by myself. I needed to see someone.

Intelligence was on the thought phone line in my head. Actually, several countries were on the line. Adversaries in fact. A war was about to begin, and we had to communicate. But I was strapped down and couldn't see any of the signals from inside the room. I was handicapped, and the damn humans wouldn't trust each other not to blow the other ones up. An attendant who had been drawing some creative art on the dry-erase message board in the common room a few hours before finally appeared in the doorway. I had commented on his creativity before the incident, and he seemed kind.

But he was all business now. I told him that I had something important to tell him. He was losing patience. He said I had thirty seconds. I asked him if he believed in Jesus Christ. He sighed, and exasperated, he sank to the floor. He wouldn't answer. I kept asking him. He moved back to the doorway and was on his way out. I asked him to touch the top of the door behind him without looking at it. I could tell that he was hesitant, and he stalled for a moment. He touched the door, and it was then that I knew we had won.

Soon after, I awoke again in a wheelchair. I was being transferred. A gentleman wheeled me into a small office and began asking me questions. I gave him my information. Then I looked down at my bracelet: "John Doe." I felt just fine, and thankfully, I would soon be at another facility. My roommate was sleeping when I arrived. The rooms there were more spacious, and the halls were cleaner. The facility even had an entertainment room with board games and a television. There was limited access to the computer and the telephone. And there were puzzles.

But the first day was a little rocky. I had still been having some lingering thoughts, and the séance was still happening. A scenario developed. There would be mass devastation and death in the near future, but it could be stopped. I walked around and did what I had to do to fix the mess. Some attendants came out and ushered me into another small room. The window looked out onto another building a ways away, but there was open space out there. That was good to see.

They sat me down on the cushioned bench and I quickly plopped down in the safe zone. One of the attendants was visibly concerned. I saw fear and confusion in her eyes. The other one was the medication lady, and she had her cart with her. I was sure she would hypnotize me if I looked directly at her, so I looked away. As I looked back, she was blinking continuously, and her eyes weren't fully visible. That was a good thing. She spoke in a calm voice with a somewhat condescending tone. But she seemed caring nevertheless. We talked for a while, and I got some more medication.

Things would stabilize quickly. I was soon transferred to a single room and felt at ease interacting with the doctors and the attendants. The social graces came back, and I was able to function again. Then my medication doctor entered the scene. He brought three young men wearing white coats along with him. They were gentlemen and professionals, and we got along. We were all on the same wavelength. The doctor seemed concerned and said that I would have to be there at least until the end of the weekend.

I still had some pressing issues to take care of, though, and the gentlemen in the white coats would help me do just that. I had to get my application to the policy school in the next day, and I had to sign the real estate transaction documents to close the sale with my father. I enlisted the help of my tech friend's younger brother to go to my apartment, find my flash drive, convert some documents, and email them to me so I could submit them to the school on time.

The lawyer who had helped us with our non-profit organization's formation was informed about the situation and was able to send someone to my apartment. I was told that they found the door wide open and the broken glass in the bathroom upstairs. I was also told later that they left a key under the mat for my friend so he could get in. He soon shot me over the documents, and I got the application in with only a few hours to spare.

My parents arrived with a CD player, my book of CDs, and eventually the real estate documents. I would sign those in a small conference room in the hospital, and the deal would be done. I would go to a few of the group meetings and was glad to have people around. The staff was accommodating, capable, and kind. We talked about nutrition in one session, played a card game in another, and talked about personal issues in yet another.

I stayed away from television time and just kept to the puzzles. I knocked a few out, and later on I found a monster. It was a globe. A full sphere. I had never seen a full-sphere jigsaw puzzle with curved pieces before. So I went to work. It was the most challenging puzzle I had ever attempted. My construction was flimsy, and every time I'd get close, another part of the globe would begin to crumble. A young lady came by, and we worked on it together for a while. But in the end, I would have to abandon the project. I would be going home that day.

CHAPTER SEVENTEEN

Tabula Rasa

THAT SAME WEEK, I went down the street with my mother and picked an evergreen out of the bunch on the lot. We placed it in a stand with some water, and I decorated it from top to bottom with some old ornaments we had kept from back in the day. I remembered that we had made some of them in grade school, and I could tell from the dust that they had been packed away for years. But I proudly displayed them nevertheless. I also added some colorful lights and finished the tree off with a huge white star on top.

The next week, I had some family over for a holiday party. It was pretty festive. I passed out some homemade soup and hot apple cider, and we talked for a few hours. I didn't feel like anything was really out of place. My uncle from my mother's side of the family had been in the hospital room with us when we signed the documents, so I knew that he knew about the situation. Nothing seemed too far off, though, and I didn't really skip too much of a beat.

The small blue pill tripled in dosage and transformed into a small, circular yellow pill, and the flaky white pill doubled in dosage as well. I began to sleep through the night, and the intensity of the thoughts subsided considerably. My functioning was getting back to almost optimal pretty quickly. A few weeks later, I would head out with my older buddies from the golf course for a quick vacation. We played several thirty-sixes and had a great time. I navigated with my tablet, and we had some good conversation over many meals out. There were only four of us, so I got to know a couple of the guys much better. But, although the whispering had died down again, the symbols were still out there. They were always out there.

Back home, I focused on the website for the organization. I worked a little more with my tech friend's brother to get the site up and running. I posted the interview, got a slideshow of some pictures going on the homepage, and wrote some content for the menu pages. I also developed a logo and made a contact database of people who I thought might be interested in our official launch. But that's about as far as I got.

Soon I would get a notice from the policy school inviting us to visit the campus and sit in on some classes. I figured that it might be a great opportunity to take a tour and to see what the lectures were like. If nothing else, it would be fun to just get a taste of what it would be like to go there. If I got in, I was planning on going, but it would still be a decision process in any case.

In the end, I decided to see for myself what was out there. I flew into the city where the school was located, which was well known for its heritage and its role in the founding of our country. I had been out there a few times in high school and college, but I never really got the chance to fully experience what the city had to offer. I was determined to do it right this time.

So I rented a car and a nice little room with a kitchenette in a brownstone on a tree-lined street. The city was just coming off the heels of a huge snowstorm, and some of the drifts were over five feet high. So driving and parking was a little difficult, but I was excited to see the city for a few days. I rode on a historic bus tour, joined a group on a themed walking tour, and even took in a ball game.

The campus was magnificent, but the classes were even better. I soaked everything in. I followed every word. I understood all of it. And it was super interesting.

"I can do this," I told myself. "I can definitely keep up with these classes. In fact, they're right up my alley. This could be something fantastic."

I left the last class on a high. I took a guided tour of the school and just walked around in the sun.

"I could get used to this," I thought.

But I would still have another month before decisions would come out.

It would be a long month, and I would try to get the website going a bit more before sending out the official launch notice. The decision came earlier than expected—I wasn't in. So I would once again have to reevaluate. I thought again about sending out the email to launch the organization, but I figured I'd pass the final decision by the board first.

My cousin mentioned that he thought the content of the website was a little thin, so I thought about it some more and eventually ended up agreeing with him wholeheartedly.

"How are people going to gravitate toward something if they don't know exactly what the activities are or how they can participate?" I thought to myself. "Some nice pictures and philosophical writings are great, but in the end, it has to pop and sizzle for people to want to get involved."

Finally, I came to the decision that a non-profit company probably wasn't the best avenue for self-expression. I still believed in my message, though. I still believed in the importance of what I had to say and its urgency in our particular moment in history. But I also understood that what I wanted to do wasn't going to work exactly like I had planned.

So I took down the website, dissolved the corporation, and donated whatever I had left in the organization's bank account to charity.

Once again, back to the drawing board. By then I had been thinking of documentary film ideas for a while. I was thinking specifically about a larger one about my parents' roots.

"I could capture their unique perspectives in a story about the origins of their families. The film could even feature a few of their close relatives. I could find all sorts of outside footage and pictures and weave something together. It would be a lot of work, but I could do it."

So I sat down and interviewed my father, my mother's brother, and my mother's cousin. They were long pieces of tape, but I felt that I could chop them up nicely.

Then I began to think of other ideas for a documentary. Some of them had to do with the concepts I had been developing for the organization.

"If I have a message here," I figured, "then the medium of film would be a great way to express that."

So I did a little digging on the web and contacted a filmmaker from a different city. I told him my story and sent him a link to the family film I made. He was gracious and took the time to watch it and to have a chat with me a little while down the road. He also introduced me to a friend of his who lived in my city and who had made the transition into documentary filmmaking himself not too long before. I would contact him soon after our chat.

I also thought of writing.

"I could write about policy issues," I thought. "I could write about personal philosophy. I could write about life."

I wrote a few pieces, but it was slow-going at first. It was hard to get motivated. Then, one day, I just sat down and stared at the galaxy on my desktop. I opened up a blank document and began to write. No planning, no notes, no structure. With just a little bit of time and a whole lot of patience, I let all of the memories pour out onto the page. I didn't try to force it. I just let it happen.

Right here, right now, at this moment in time, I'm thinking to myself, "Are beginnings really relevant after all?"

You bet they are.

ABOUT THE AUTHOR

DARA SANANDAJI graduated from Dartmouth College in 2000, where he earned a B.A. in Economics and studied abroad at the University Autónoma de Madrid. He then graduated from Chicago-Kent College of Law in 2006 and later worked in the financial services sector, where he earned his Certified Financial Planner (CFP ®) designation in 2011. A few years later, Dara transitioned into writing and filmmaking, and since then, he has written, directed, and produced two feature-length documentary films. Dara has also authored the title *Mirror for the Mind: A Tribute to the Wisdom of Humanity*, and he hosted his own independent radio show, "The Big Picture Radio Show," in Chicago in 2014.

www.ingramcontent.com/pod-product-compliance
Ingram Content Group UK Ltd.
Pitfield, Milton Keynes, MK11 3LW, UK
UKHW021935200726
13853UKWH00011B/2140